THE WHITE-COLLAR SHUFFLE

THE WHITE-COLLAR SHUFFLE

Who Does What in Today's Computerized Workplace

RICHARD W. LARSON
AND DAVID J. ZIMNEY

amacom

AMERICAN MANAGEMENT ASSOCIATION

Library of Congress Cataloging-in-Publication Data

Larson, Richard W.
    The white-collar shuffle : who does what in today's computerized
    workplace / Richard W. Larson, David J. Zimney
        p. cm.
    Includes bibliographical references.
    ISBN 0-8144-5996-X
        1. Office practice—Automation.   2. Labor
productivity.   3. White collar workers.   4. Organizational
effectiveness.   I. Zimney, David J., 1946- .
    II. Title.
    HF5548.L28   1990   89-81024
    651.8—dc20   CIP

Printing number

10   9   8   7   6   5   4   3   2   1

Contents

Preface

This is not a technical book, however, no one should invest in office automation without first reading it. More importantly, do not put it down until you have tested its theory for yourself. If your company is pursuing the elusive "white-collar productivity" butterfly, then you owe it to management and to yourself to consider the ideas presented here. Some of our facts are startling; many of the ideas are revolutionary. Most managers and executives are oblivious to these concepts or only dimly aware of their significance. Nevertheless, this may be the only way American business will successfully compete in tomorrow's increasingly competitive world markets.

This is not a technical book, but it does talk about technology. That is because technology in the office—call it integrated office systems, decision support systems, end-user computing, or whatever—is the ticket to future productivity. The choices are not clear cut and mistakes can be costly. No office technology can compensate for shortsighted management and hazy objectives. Yes, the book talks about technology, but it is really about effective management!

Professionals on all levels of management will find these ideas stimulating. Top managers will see them as a blueprint for attaining their strategic business objectives. Information Systems personnel will better understand the problems and challenges of the services they offer and find the way to emerge as a powerful new force in the corporation. The growing number of department managers will see in this book a way to justify their investment in productivity-boosting equipment and software, and discover new means for organizing work or gaining support from I/S organizations. Personnel managers will find their human resources concerns resolved, so they can more successfully meet the needs of the nineties. Information Systems vendors will discover new customer needs in what they assumed was a mature market. In fact, they could benefit handsomely by organizing their product designs around the concepts presented here. Educators will welcome the comprehensive approach to white-collar productivity and the objective look at the nature of work itself.

This book is in basically two parts. Part I presents our observations on the nature of work and the proper allocation of different kinds of work. We then offer our proposal for an integrated office software system that enhances the creative work of American business's highest paid individuals, its management and professional personnel. Information is powerful, so we look at the Information Systems services function and propose a new management structure that facilitates maximum use of today's technology. The heart of our proposal is a management revolution, a new way to structure work and responsibility to promote greater product and service innovation. Our trail-blazing management approach works, as shown in Part II, which consists of seven case studies that prove the validity of Work Redistribution Management.

It is time to downsize obsolete corporate bureaucracies by redistributing work itself, and not just eliminating people. It is time to awaken the brain power that lies dormant and accelerate change for competitive advantage. This is not a technical book, but with it you will better understand how to use information technology to leverage your most important assets: people and creativity.

R.W.L.
D.J.Z.

A Special Thanks

Peter Karp is the president of Business Science International, a market research firm in Englewood Cliffs, New Jersey. Peter has been a close personal friend over the years and has been an advocate of the Work Redistribution Management (WRM) technique.

Peter is excellent at helping organizations identify creative opportunities through "creative research strategies" to determine if creative opportunities are real opportunities.

The second special thanks goes to Jeffrey H. Tucker. Dr. Tucker was attracted to the WRM process during his tenure at Georgia State University while we were implementing the technique in one of the university's departments. Dr. Tucker has also become a very close friend and continues to be involved in assisting us with further studies.

Introduction

An executive of a large international company recently announced that work elimination had become a survival issue. He explained, "Outdated tasks have to be eliminated. If they aren't, we won't remain competitive." The areas targeted for improvement ranged from requirements definition and development lead times to procedures for announcing new products, more efficient logistics, automated manufacturing systems, and a streamlined planning process. Nearly all of these concerned white-collar productivity. Sounds impressive! However, none of the plans reflected an understanding of the white-collar productivity problem. The approach was to encourage employees to change their work habits to "simplify" the way they work, eliminate unnecessary tasks, and streamline business procedures. Of course, there was a common edict that appeared logical but was not: No more administrative or secretarial support personnel could be hired without the highest executive approval. Only temporary people could be hired, and even that would require a major effort.

Soliciting suggestions from employees as to what work should be eliminated may be helpful but it is a management cop-out. There is no excuse or substitute for recognizing the white-collar productivity challenge and developing a long-term plan. These limp efforts are analogous to putting a Band-Aid on a cancerous tumor. Such measures only delay the inevitable surgery.

These desperate actions come about because executives are frustrated. They are frustrated with the accelerated pace of changing international markets, with demands for innovative products and services, and with increasingly competitive pressures. They are slashing their professional staffs through incentives such as early retirement and attractive severance packages, or simply releasing these excess personnel into the unemployment pool.

Unfortunately, programs designed to thin the professional ranks often leave companies stripped of their most creative individuals.

This international company directed its employees to question what they do and how they do it. That demonstrated executive sensitivity to the vast energy wasted on unnecessary work. But the real answer starts with a reevaluation of white-collar work itself, and realization of why current organizational structures and segmental management attitudes force professionals to work ineffectively.

During the last two generations, the labor distribution in our economy has changed dramatically. In 1900, there were about 29 million people employed in the United States and 37 percent were farmers. In 1985, about 107 million people were employed and less than 3 percent were farmers. Those 3 percent are so productive, we pay them to put their land into a "soil bank."

During this same period, the number of blue-collar workers increased but their percentage of the work force actually decreased from 36 to 28 percent. As a result of these changes, seven of every ten workers today are classified as white-collar or service sector employees.

If U.S. companies compete internationally, executives must increase the productivity of people who spend their day in an office. These 40 million workers constitute 37 percent of the work force and are the majority of highly paid employees.

Productivity is no longer measured simply as output of goods and services versus labor input. Now "multifaceted productivity" measures changes in output owing to new technologies, economies of scale, alterations in the experience and education of labor, capacity utilization rates, and organization of production in addition to just capital and labor. While the definition of productivity has grown, many managers have continued to focus on efficiency to justify speed and automation. Unfortunately, they have tried to apply the productivity principles of the assembly line to the office environment. The result has been only slightly short of a disaster.

Specifically, managers have used technology to increase the *efficiency* of administrative and clerical support people. Automation has enhanced word processing, accounting, bookkeeping, payroll, shipping, production, and procurement. Technology investments have been justified through either a reduction in the number of clerical support people or an increase in their work volume. Is efficiency the right focus for measuring white-collar productivity in the 90s? Is efficiency the right basis for investing in "office" technology? We do not think so!

Attempts to increase white-collar productivity with traditional "office automation" generally have failed. The excuses cited include no equipment connectivity, software incompatibility, lack of proper training, no management involvement, and so on. These are important issues, but they are not the reason why technology has delivered lackluster productivity results.

Some managers, including data processing professionals, claim today's office solutions are not complete, not mature, not fully integrated, and not easy to learn. There is some truth to these claims. Assume for a moment that 1995 office technology is available today and end-user training budgets were doubled. Most companies would still miss the competitive boat when investing in high-tech systems. The answer to increased white-collar productivity lies in defining an additional management approach to restructuring white-collar work. It involves changing the organizational support structure itself. It means designing and delivering augmentation tools, enhancing worker skills, and changing the way people are managed. To understand this, we must *first* take a fresh look at office work and how it supports the business objectives. *Second*, we must learn to distinguish between different types of work in the office environment and what we really pay people to do, versus what they do today. *Third*, we must have a long-range plan of how we want the people, equipment, and procedures to change to support more high-value work. *Fourth,* the organizational structure must be modified so we can consistently deliver the right work to the right people with the right resources to accomplish it. *Fifth,* we must have a new approach to analyzing, redistributing, and managing work and people.

Business leaders today instinctively know something is wrong and they realize money and technology alone cannot fix it. Too often, quick fixes for business problems are implemented with a "production efficiency" mentality that focuses on automation. If automation will not cut operating expenses, drastic measures to reduce salary expenses are undertaken. The rule is: *Reducing costs is king, so if you cannot automate, cut the headcount.*

In 1987 alone, we saw a number of large companies reduce their ranks of white-collar professionals and managers. For example, General Motors' publicly reported goal was to slash its salaried work force by 25 percent and eliminate base pay raises for 110,000 salaried workers. Chrysler announced similar cost-cutting steps, reducing white-collar employment by about 9.5 percent, or 3,600 workers, by the end of 1987. IBM took some uncharacteristic steps to cut expenses by reducing its work force by 15,000 employees, mostly staff professionals and managers, through early retirement and other incentive programs. Mellon Bank announced a plan to cut about 2,000 jobs. Chemical Bank New York announced a major reorganization that eliminated about 2,100 jobs in its Chemical Bank subsidiary.

Today's complex business problems need the combined efforts of the brightest, most experienced minds. When leading companies eliminate layers of white-collar professionals and managers, are they releasing their best, their brightest individuals? Unfortunately, some executives neither know nor care. Their objective is not to weed out the unproductive but rather to reduce headcount to the point where only critical business activities survive. But is that what happens?

In the next ten years, companies will use more severance incentives or layoffs to quickly adjust their balance sheets and streamline their organizations. Sometimes these reductions will only eliminate excessive layers of a redundant management system that simply filters and relays information, and which can be accomplished better with today's electronic communications. Even these actions often are financially shortsighted. After the headcount is reduced, much of the same work remains to be done. The best individuals have departed and the remaining people have even less time for creative work. Downsizing has made secretaries out of professionals!

While it remains important to invest in capital equipment for more efficient production and assembly-line operations, it is now time for a company's investment priorities to leverage its most valuable asset: brain power. Harnessing the creative energy in an organization encourages more creative work. That is only part of the answer. Gaining a competitive edge in the 1990s starts with understanding the new office environment. The following chapters clarify the financial opportunities, the needs, the solutions, and the new analysis that should be the basis for upcoming investments in technology. More important, this analysis will give management the information it needs, on a continuing basis, to restructure the organization as work and priorities in the business change.

We have been talking about the problems of customers of technology vendors, but some technology companies are even more frustrated. Their traditional market opportunity has matured and their salespeople are unable to communicate the reasons why management should invest in their technology and software. Traditional markets for their technology were the predictable business applications such as order entry, billing, payroll, inventory control, purchasing and material requirements planning, demand deposits, mortgage loan accounting, patient admissions and billing, policy tracking, actuarial accounting, to name just a few. Obviously, some small and medium-size companies are still automating these activities. Few vendors fully realize the largest opportunity: to provide productivity tools to white-collar professionals. Chapter 5 concentrates on this problem, but all aspects of this book reinforce this potential.

The benefits to be derived from integrated office systems have been poorly explained and documented by vendors and end users. This is because most vendors, data processing professionals, and departmental managers fail to grasp the key ingredients of the picture: the nature of work, the needs of people, the potential of the technology, and the procedures for monitoring productivity. The justification will continue to be elusive until the principles set forth in the pages that follow are put into practice. Businesses have been so busy "computerizing" work that they have forgotten what it is. So we begin by reevaluating the basic concepts of work, then apply them to the goal of heightened productivity and increased innovation.

PART I
The Productivity Dilemma—and Its Solution

Chapter 1

All Office Work
Is Not the Same

The office environment is not a factory, and a professional's productivity cannot be measured in widgets per hour. Traditional attempts to measure white-collar productivity quickly become unworkable. Yet there is an answer to this problem. Before delving into the subtleties of creative and routine work, however, we need to be sure we are talking the same language. This first chapter presents a handful of business terms, with precise definitions that may sometimes differ from what you are used to. It is essential that you adopt these meanings now so you can follow the arguments presented in later chapters. It is in this initial chapter that we also discuss the nature of work today and show how it falls into three basic categories: routine, creative, and reactive.

The Basics

The evolution of data processing and word processing has fostered a misunderstanding of the term *office*. In its simplest form, it is usually associated with word processing and copy machines. "Office" should refer simply to what it is: a work environment. This is how we will use the word in this book.

Likewise, all *work* accomplished in an office consists of activities and applications.

For example, if you are painting a picture, the brush strokes are the activity and the resulting picture is the application. Examples of *activities* performed in the office include:

- Meetings
- Copying papers
- Working with data
- Handling mail
- Transmitting written material (distribution)
- Answering or making telephone calls
- Filing papers
- Working with text
- Managing or supervising others
- Proofing typed materials
- Working with graphics
- Sorting and assembling papers

When a number of activities or applications in a department or division become routine, we call these a *business process*. For example, suppose Maria goes to a file drawer or a computer file and retrieves the account history on the ABC Company. She looks at credits and debits, and calculates or directs the computer to calculate a new total. The calculation indicates the ABC account has an accounts receivable total of $3,567.54. Maria then types the accounts receivable document or has the computer print the document. These activities and the resulting document constitute the accounts receivable business process. Each step taken is an activity, and the resulting documents are the applications within the accounts receivable business process.

Examples of other business *applications* are:

- Letters
- Proposals
- Inventory lists
- Accounts payable
- Purchase orders
- Presentations

- General ledgers
- Invoices
- Reference manuals
- Flowcharts
- Drawings
- Memos
- Sales plans
- Price lists
- Parts lists
- Reports
- Travel expense forms
- Computer printouts
- Bills
- Time cards
- Phone directories
- Forecasts

Applications, if produced, are the final stage of an activity or business process. Notice that posting data to the general ledger is an activity, but the general ledger itself is an application.

Some business applications have become basic data processing activities and applications, including order entry, inventory control, payroll, billing, accounts payable, general ledger, invoicing, accounts receivable, and sales analysis. It is interesting to note that all of these applications are accomplished in an *office*. In fact many data processing managers claim they are *not* responsible for "office systems," because these operations are considered *business applications*, not *office applications*. Why? Many business managers respond, "Because office applications are mainly word processing."

It is true that word processing is an activity accomplished in an office. Both data processing and word processing support certain activities with machines that automate the high-volume, predictable, repetitive steps in certain business applications. So why aren't all applications accomplished in an office referred to as *office applications*? Unfortunately, some people still perceive that the word "office" applies only to word processing, photocopying, or electronic mail.

Data processing today typically refers to "numbers" processing and the applications that result. Most information stored in computers is data, or numeric information, but "data," when used in its generic sense, means all formats: numbers, text, graphics, voice, annotations, signatures, and handwriting. In this book, *data* is used in its broader meaning to refer to all formats. When numbers are meant, they are referred to as *numbers (data)* format.

Understanding how people work together in logical groups is an important ingredient to understanding the nature of work, the technology needed to support it, and the benefits it affords. *Work group* is a term used to indicate the smallest identifiable element in an organization with a common manager and whose members share a common objective with a strong need to communicate among themselves. For example, a typical work group may consist of 15 people: 12 principals or staff professionals and 2 support (clerical/administrative personnel) reporting to a manager. A work group is always composed of both principals and support personnel, and includes a manager.

Some companies have staff professionals working for one manager while the secretarial and clerical support personnel report to a second manager. This organizational structure reflects the lack of understanding some executives have about work and how to increase white-collar productivity. It also is one of the reasons why many secretaries feel they are not part of the office team and are underutilized.

Two new terms have been introduced: principals and support personnel. *Principals* consist of the following categories of workers:

Management Examples

- Chief executive officer
- President
- Vice presidents
- Directors
- Managers

Non-Management Examples

- Professionals
- Engineers
- Scientists

- Technicians
- Sales/marketing personnel

In 1900, there were fewer than 3 million office workers classified as principals; by 1985, there were 24 million office principals.

The second group, *support personnel*, has been the victim of pruning shears, most often to justify the cost of routine automation.

Support Personnel Examples

- Secretaries
- Stenographers
- Clerical workers
- Receptionists
- Librarians
- Typists
- Bookkeepers
- Office machine operators
- Telephone operators
- Data entry operators

There were fewer than 1 million office support personnel in 1900; in 1985, there were about 16 million support personnel. Of these 16 million, approximately 4 million were secretaries. We discuss principal-to-secretary ratios later on, but the national average of 24 million principals supported by 4 million secretaries gives us a 6:1 ratio nationally.

How People Work

Some myths have accumulated over the years relative to work in the office environment. We can debunk them by exploring the "obvious" answers to the following questions:

1. How do you and I work in an office environment?
2. Does your current system support your working needs?
3. How should office technology support the way people work?

The answers may seem apparent, but in fact they are not. Managers making office investment decisions fail to see that they are simultaneously making decisions about business problems which could restructure the office work, office personnel, and office organization.

Ask yourself the following: Which principal-to-support ratio shown below is generally best?

Principal	:	Support
1	:	1
3	:	1
5	:	1
7	:	1
10	:	1

Most managers respond that a 10:1 ratio is best for the organization because it is the most efficient. In fact, most people believe that the higher the ratio (i.e., 10:1, 15:1, 20:1, etc.), the better.

Now look at the ratios in a different light. Consider the relationship between the average principal's salary and the average support person's salary. For the purpose of this discussion, we use two average salaries, principals at $50,000 per year and support personnel at $20,000. (Substitute your salary figures for ours if they are different; the actual salaries are not what's important. What is important is the message they impart when used in this format. The one relationship that stands from one company to another is that principals' salaries appear to average two to two and a half times those

of support personnel.) Apply this to the ratios and ask
yourself which is best:

Principal	:	Support
$ 50,000	:	$20,000
$150,000	:	$20,000
$250,000	:	$20,000
$350,000	:	$20,000
$500,000	:	$20,000

The underlying myth is that only one type of work exists
in any business—routine work. Since equipment replaces
support personnel in the accomplishment of routine work,
the cost of equipment is justified by reductions in support
personnel, and the result has continued to be higher principal-to-support ratios. Doesn't this give you some cause for
concern? As an executive, manager, or professional staff
person, ask yourself: Are there tasks you perform that could
be accomplished by a support person who is paid 40 percent
of your salary? If you answer yes, and it happens on a
frequent basis, then you are not getting a balanced return
on your investment in human resources.

Here is another question: How do you differentiate
between the activities and responsibilities of office workers?

You might respond that the differences are clearly documented in their job descriptions or their performance
plans. Few organizations practice differentiation of job responsibilities on a daily basis. Just ask your professional staff
how much of its time is wasted doing work that a good
secretary or administrative person could perform. It is not
simply a matter of getting rid of unnecessary work. It is
getting the right work to the right people. Most business
organizations do not have a management approach to ensure
that the right person performs the right job.

The heart of the problem rests with traditional organizational structure and the inherent assumption that the

structure is correct and complete. Today's standard organizational structure needs to be modified. Consider your answers to the following questions:

1. *Does all the work you perform have the same degree of difficulty?* Everyone usually responds the same: no. This implies that there is a range of difficulty for all work accomplished in the office.

2. Assuming the range of difficulty is represented on a continuum with two extremes, *what words would you use to describe those two extremes?* Meaningful terms that identify these work extremes are difficult to find. *Creative* and *routine* are suggested in Figure 1-1.

3. *What are the differences between routine and creative work?* Routine work consists of highly repetitive activities that can easily accommodate large volumes, have a high frequency of use, and, therefore, are predictable. Creative work has a one-of-a-kind appearance and is low volume, infrequent, and of a first-time nature.

4. *What are the key characteristics of routine work?* Routine work exists in every office. It occurs frequently enough to be reduced to a set of written procedures that explain the who, what, when, where, how, and why of the activity and its application. The following description is an example of a routine business process:

Figure 1-1. The structure of work.

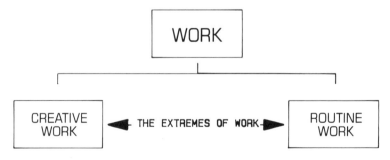

The problem: You have moved to a different state and you must apply for a new driver's license.

Who:	You
What:	Need a new driver's license
When:	Sometime after moving into your new home
Where:	Probably at the State Department of Motor Vehicles
How:	Call the Motor Vehicle Department and learn its procedure
Why:	In order not to break local laws

The solution: You follow the proper procedure.

Who:	All applicants
What:	Apply for a new driver's license
When:	Within 90 days of moving to the state
Where:	At the Department of Motor Vehicles
How:	Wait in line, fill out form, and take written test (on a machine, preprogrammed); a passing score of 70, automatically graded by the machine, means you fill out a computer form, have your picture taken; license arrives within 30 days, computer adds you to state records automatically and deletes license in old state
Why:	Because you cannot drive in the new state without a current license

This is a simple, repetitive, predictable activity with volume and written procedures. It is easy to train people to perform each task, to delegate these activities, and to make the process efficient. Volume and repetition justify the cost of automating such a business process.

5. What are the key characteristics of creative work? Creative work is at the opposite extreme. The creative energy must flow before any valuable business process can be devel-

oped. When the need for a driver's license was first recognized, creative effort was required. The business problem looked a little different:

Who:	Should everyone who drives an automobile have one?
What:	What privileges are given with a driver's license? What should it look like? Should operators have it with them at all times? What information should be on it? What if the motorists disobey the law?
When:	When should people be allowed to drive? When do we give people a license? Do they need to learn to drive first? Should they have a permit to learn?
Where:	Where does a person get a license? Is it a county, state, or federal license?
Why:	Why do we need to govern people's driving?
How:	How will this program be funded? How can information be transferred when people move? How can the need for a license be enforced? How much is the fee?

In the creative process, answers to such questions are developed for the first time to provide an ultimate business process that will consist of activities and applications. In the beginning, there are no rules or directions to follow. The answers are unknown. Once the activities are developed and defined, repetition and volume transform those creative activities and applications into a business process. In doing creative work, people evaluate a potential business need and look for answers. This is a first-time effort.

The Creative Work Process

While there are no specific rules governing creative work, there is a commonality as to how to approach it. Once you understand the different stages in the creative process, you can see how it is possible to enhance those first-time creative efforts. Ask yourself the following questions in relation to creative work you perform:

1. *What do you do first to define, develop, and understand an idea or problem?* Most people answer "research." They attempt to gather information. Thus, the first stage of the creative process is to look for relevant information.

2. *What do you do with information once you have found it?* Most people mull the information over in their minds. They make notes and rethink the opportunity. They store the information, analyze it (network it with other data), and start to draw conclusions that can be shaped into a pattern which can be communicated: a math theorem, a set of musical notes, a graph, a speech, and soon they create something for the first time, and that creative product may either stand alone or may be part of a larger solution to a problem.

Let us look at some office activities and determine how these terms are used.

Principals Keyboard, Secretaries Type

People sometimes confuse making notes with word processing. Since the mid-1960s, word processing has become associated with secretaries and clerical support personnel; there is an illusion that only secretaries work with words. Principals document their thoughts and research with notes, outlines, and rough drafts. This function is called *document preparation* and principals do what is called *keyboarding*. Secretaries, on the other hand, perform *document processing*, more widely known as word processing or typing. The two words refer to the same activity, so why use both? There is a major difference between these two aspects of work. Document preparation is required in the creative or development phase. Document processing is the activity required in the production or the routine phase.

Revision, Part of the Creative Process

Principals often depend on secretaries to type drafts, which are subject to further change, but support personnel generally become very upset when a manager or professional makes revisions to a typed document. After all, revision is a key part of document preparation, a part of the creative process. Unfortunately, many principals assume they can use word processing centers for creative work. Conversely, many secretaries erroneously assume that once they are asked to process a document, the creative work is finished.

Creative vs. Routine Work

Viewing work in terms of its routine and creative aspects helps to define the nature of the work and identify who should accomplish which phase, allowing the right work to get to the right person. For example, what work could you delegate to someone to handle while you are on vacation? If you can delegate work to a subordinate, peer, or support person, most likely it is routine, not creative. If the work cannot be delegated, it is probably creative. Can you define the who, what, when, where, how, and why of a particular business problem or challenge? Can you define these same variables for the solution? If the answer is yes, the work is likely routine.

Do you know when the work is due? If it has a regular, recurring date, the work is usually routine. Creative work can also have a due date, as in the case of a customer proposal, the engineering blueprints for a new building, and so on. Have you done this work before, or is it a first-time effort? If you have done the work before, especially on a fairly regular basis, the work is routine. Do you know where to look for the answer to the problem? If you do and the answer is intuitive, the activity may be routine. If you are unsure of the solution process and the answer is not intuitive, then the activity may be creative.

What about training and educational experience? Assume you (or a new employee) are given a new job which requires you to use a personal computer and a spreadsheet software package. You have never used a personal computer or the software. Your employer recommends that you take the time to go through a self-study tutorial. The activity of using the tutorial to learn the personal computer and spreadsheet program may be creative because most learning experiences tend to be a creative process.

Some More Terminology

Many times other words are used to describe routine and creative work, words like "automation," "augmentation," "efficiency," "effectiveness," and "innovation." Let us put these words into perspective.

Automation

Very few people challenge the need for payroll, order entry, billing, accounts receivable, accounts payable, inventory control, general ledger, and other traditional business applications. If the work has value, volume, and repetition, Information Systems (data processing) can apply technology to produce the application faster and cheaper. The results are a well-defined, operational business process, and the best way of accomplishing this work is with the assistance of *automation*.

In its formal sense, automation is "the automatic operation or control of a process, equipment, or a system." To understand this definition, you need two other definitions. A *process* is a system of operations used in the production of something. It is a series of actions, changes, or functions that bring about an end or result. A *system* is a group of interacting, interrelated, or interdependent elements forming a complex whole.

An informal definition of automation is "the mechanization of a predictable set of activities to minimize resources (time, energy, money) required." The key to successful automation is a repetitive set of activities with volume. Heavy volume is usually needed to justify the equipment investment necessary to mechanize the business process.

Augmentation

Working with an idea is usually a first-time effort, resulting in a volume of one. Automation, therefore, is not an accurate term to apply to this effort. *Augmentation* is the ability to increase or to make your capacity greater, as in extent, function, quantity, or quality. When an office worker accomplishes any activity for the first time, there is no automation program to assist owing to the fact that there is no volume or repetition. In this case the business must augment the worker's efforts. We discuss the implications of augmentation later in this chapter.

Efficiency

Many business people use the terms "efficiency," "effectiveness," and "innovation" interchangeably, but they do not mean the same thing. The rationale for promoting automation of routine work is increased efficiency.

The dictionary definition of efficiency is "the ability to provide the effect wanted without waste of time, energy, etc." We shorten the definition to "doing things faster."

Efficiency reduces the time wasted on activities in the production of something, therefore, the cost to produce an item is reduced for a given volume. As volume increases, cost decreases. Two common objectives for automation are higher volume and lower cost.

Effectiveness

Modifying an existing business process, a set of activities, or an application in a way that positively impacts performance is *effectiveness*. The dictionary defines "effective" as "producing the desired effect." We refine the definition to "doing things better!"

Normally, creative efforts in a business environment are undertaken to solve perceived or actual problems or to meet known challenges. The results may be used to modify and improve existing products or services or to improve performance. When a creative effort improves an existing set of activities and applications, this is effectiveness.

After repeatedly accomplishing the same activities over a long period, you may think of a better, faster, more accurate, more productive way to achieve the same or better results. You take that "first-time" idea and refine it into an activity or application and effectiveness is the result. The term effectiveness is used specifically to mean creatively modifying an existing application or activity. Only after the modification has been put into practice can the process again be made more efficient.

Innovation

In contrast to effectiveness, *innovation* means conceiving and developing an entirely new application or activity. The term is used to describe a truly first-time activity or application. Innovation is the creative conception and execution of an intuitive need.

To clarify the distinction here, think of two typical innovations: a doctoral thesis, and a unique and different entrepreneurial effort. The doctoral thesis is, by definition, a new idea—something no one has written about before. By our definition, there are two types of doctoral theses—an effective thesis and an innovative thesis. An effective thesis is one that expands on basic ideas already known or in practice. An innovative thesis is one that most people would describe as a totally new theory or concept.

The second example is illustrated by the Federal Express Corporation. Fred Smith's new idea was that people would pay a premium to transport articles faster than the U.S. mail or other services. He risked millions on this simple idea and it became a reality. That is innovation. In short, innovation is "doing new or better things!"

How do these terms apply to creative and routine work? Routine work strives for efficiency. Through automation, efficiency is enhanced by word processors and data processors when sufficient volume is present. Creative work strives for effectiveness by modifying an existing application or set of activities. Through innovation, creative effort conceives and develops new business processes, activities, or applications. Figure 1-2 attempts to summarize how we feel these terms should be used in any business.

The terms creative, reactive, and routine tend to be words used to express work in the idea and accomplishment stages, or before the fact. Innovation, effectiveness, and efficiency tend to be words used to express reaction to work after the fact. Businesses have the opportunity to augment creative work and automate routine work.

Reactive Work

Do you have the same amount of time to respond to all your work? Obviously not. There is a third type of work that

Figure 1-2. The relationship among key terms.

WORK EVOLUTION

we just alluded to—reactive work that is time sensitive (see Figure 1-3).

Reactive work is not anticipated or planned. It is externally imposed and it is disruptive. For example, suppose your manager comes into your office five minutes before lunch and says, "The meeting we had scheduled with the vice president next Friday is this afternoon at one o'clock. Be ready!" If you are already prepared and know the answers to the vice president's concerns, this meeting would be a *reactive-routine* event for you. If you have to create material and haven't yet had time to do so, this would be a *reactive-creative* situation. Depending on the amount of reaction time needed to prepare a response, the most you may be able to do is present an outline of ideas that may solve a problem.

As a result, many people refer to reactive work in two ways, reactive-routine and reactive-creative. Some aspects of reactive work can be delegated if the time compression is not too great. Consider the following two phone calls. First, a customer calls you, the sales manager. You happen to know the customer personally. The customer wishes to place an order for an existing product the company has ordered many times before. This time the customer wants to change

Figure 1-3. Reactive work in the structure of work.

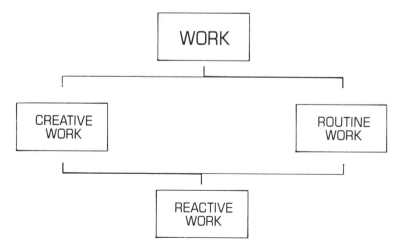

the color, double the quantity, and have it delivered tomorrow. A change in the terms from C.O.D. to payment within 30 days is also requested. Your activities are disrupted, there is a sense of urgency, but when you think about all the requests, they fall within established business procedures, even the terms of payment. So this is a reactive-routine situation—a normal situation with the time compressed. The compression is not so severe that you cannot delegate this reactive-routine call to your sales representative.

After the first customer finishes, a second customer calls. A secretary advises you that the customer's corporate attorney wants "to chat with you for just a moment." After a long silence, you pick up the phone and the attorney advises you that tomorrow you will be formally notified of that company's intention to file a $2 million lawsuit against you and your company. This would be a reactive-creative situation and would be a first-time, one-of-a-kind challenge.

The Dynamics of Work and Productivity

Many business people think the secret to greater productivity is simply getting people to work faster, but this is false. To understand the relationship between speed and productivity, ask a group of individuals to continuously write their signatures on a piece of paper for two minutes. Then, ask them to write their signature for an additional two minutes, this time as fast as possible. The only criterion is that their signatures be legible. Meanwhile, write the figure "13%" somewhere on a piece of paper, blackboard, or easel where it can't be seen. Ask each individual to calculate the percentage of additional signatures written the second time, using the following formula:

$$\frac{\text{Total 2}}{\text{Total 1}} = xx\%$$

List their answers on a blackboard and then reveal your answer. Surprisingly, most will be 13 percent! If this exercise is repeated over the course of 30 minutes, the percent will increase slightly and then taper off, stabilizing near the 13 percent. Just encouraging people to accomplish something routine faster will not achieve meaningful, lasting increases in productivity.

In the blue-collar environment, encouragement has been replaced by an unforgiving assembly line that moves at a preset pace around the shop floor area. Some managers have attempted to apply this same logic to white-collar work by designing a web of segmented routine activities. It has not worked because of a basic premise of this book: All work is not the same.

The nature of work is dynamic, not static. It changes from creative to routine, through repetition. To illustrate how work changes over time, try this exercise, using the following diagram:

```
┌─────────────────────────┐
│  1    5                  │
│    13        14  4  2    │
│     3        16          │
│    15  17      18  6     │
│                          │
│    23  9       10        │
│   7  21            12    │
│       11       24  20    │
│   19           22    8   │
└─────────────────────────┘
```

Let us assume that the above diagram represents an overhead view of the work location within four walls of a business. All the essential procedures necessary to order products, make and ship them to a customer, and invoice and collect the money are performed here. Ask each member of a group to connect the sequential steps (numbers) on the chart, then stop the group after 30 seconds and determine the highest number connected.

Obviously, people's performance would improve if they walked around inside the building each day and became familiar with the procedures. Doing this the first time is a creative activity. A first-time learning activity requires creative skills to define and understand the procedure. Now let us assume that it is six months later. Through repetitive performance and job experience, the person has become familiar with the procedural steps and has increased his or her speed in connecting the numbers. From a learning viewpoint, the activity has slowly converted from a creative challenge to a routine task.

To expedite the learning, show the person what he or she has learned in the past six months. The following diagram shows the structure behind the organization—the method by which the numbers are laid out:

Odd	Even	
1 5 13 3 15 17	14 4 2 16 18 6	Numbers 1–6, 13–18, etc.
23 9 7 21 11 19	10 12 24 20 22 8	Numbers 7–12, 19–24, etc.

The odd numbers are all on the left side of the page; the even numbers are all on the right. The first six numbers (1 to 6) are in the top half; the second six (7 to 12) are in the bottom half. This sequence repeats itself with the third group of six numbers (13 to 18) in the top of the page and the fourth group (19 to 24) in the bottom half. Over time, the repetition of the activity has stored the pattern in our long-term memory, so that the work has changed from a creative problem to a routine task.

After accomplishing an activity many times, most principals are ready to delegate tasks to new employees and train them on the system. Does knowledge of the steps affect productivity? To test this, ask the individual to once again connect the numbers in the diagram.

```
1    5
   13        14  4  2
    3        16
  15 17      18  6

  23  9      10
 7 21            12
    11       24 20
 19          22   8
```

After 30 seconds, stop and ask that person to compute the productivity gain:

$$\frac{\text{Second try}}{\text{First try}} = xx\%$$

Normally, people experience a 150 to 300 percent productivity improvement. That's quite good when compared to the 13 percent increase achieved by working faster.

As people gain experience in a job, ultimately the steps required to perform that job become clear. If you carry the example to its ultimate conclusion, once all activities are defined and routinized, they are now ready to be sequenced chronologically. If the activities and application involved have sufficient volume and frequent use, they receive the benefit of automation through systematization. When work has volume, the automation effort is paid for in the efficiency achieved. This is as true in an office environment as it is in the factory.

Automation and Augmentation Technology

To evaluate new equipment for office work, a manager must understand the work, the people, and the procedures so as to distinguish between automation and augmentation needs.

In routine work, automated computer procedures generally have preference over people requirements. For example, the efficient, routine production of a large volume of accurate paychecks would have priority over employees' desired methods or approaches; the resulting efficiency justifies the means.

Creative office work is different. Since it is, by definition, concerned with first-time activities, so the software that augments creative efforts cannot be rigid. It must be flexible to accommodate the way people work creatively. It must be a tool that enhances the creative process. The software must allow individuals to follow their work sequence naturally, the way people work. To better understand why this is so important, let us take a closer look at the relationship among ideas, applications, and activities.

As an idea develops in a business, it generates activities such as meetings and discussions, which usually result in notes being taken. Notes, outlines, and rough drafts often lead to an overhead projector presentation or a draft document describing new business concepts. The draft is ultimately finalized, published, and distributed. A system in any office environment must be designed to accommodate all stages of the process, as well as permit the transfer of work among the principals, support personnel, and, ultimately, the systems used in the office when the characteristics of the work are applicable.

Managers need to understand the evolutionary process of office work. In purchasing technology, they must recognize how an idea is transformed from creative work into a routine activity or application. Figure 1-4 shows the evolutionary process of office work.

Augmentation

So, how does augmentation help office workers? It is possible to augment creative efforts involving a first-time

Figure 1-4. The evolutionary process of work.

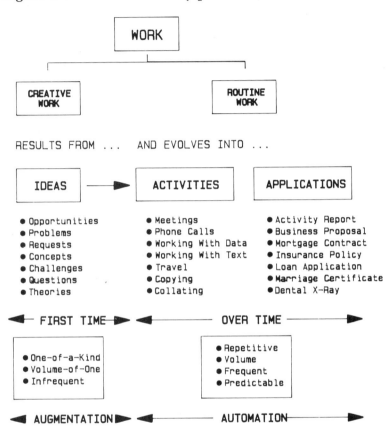

activity, but not possible to automate these efforts. Here is a quick example: What method (mental, longhand, calculator, spreadsheet, computer program) would you use to accomplish each of the following?

Multiply 9 × 20
Multiply 689 × 9
Multiply $23,978,587 × 1.948637

Most people would use mental, longhand, or a calculator, in that order. If you use a calculator, is that automation?

As the task gets harder to perform mentally, we augment our mental capabilities with tools such as a pad and pencil, calculator, personal computer, and so on.

Why longhand for the second calculation, and a calculator for the third? The second problem was simple. The third problem would take the average person four to five minutes to accomplish in longhand, another four to five minutes to check the process, and the probability of error is high. The calculator saved time—six to ten seconds versus eight to ten minutes. The advantages of the calculator are obvious: greater productivity, more accuracy, and a tedious activity made simple. Is the use of the calculator automation? In the strictest sense of the word, yes. "Automation" is from the Greek word *automatos*, which means "akin to the way your mind works" or "self-acting." We gave a simple definition earlier in the chapter, but here is a fuller explanation. Automation is the use of a machine or mechanism designed to follow a predetermined and repetitive sequence of operations by responding to encoded instructions as a substitute for human effort, observation, or decision making.

After you enter the numbers, the calculator retrieves them from memory and multiplies them when the "times" key is depressed. The multiplication is "automatic," but most people would not call this automation; the term appears to be overkill. How about augmentation? Earlier in the chapter we described it as the use of something or someone to increase your capacity or capability as to size, extent, accuracy, ease, quantity, or quality. Augmentation appears to be a better description of our use of the calculator.

When accomplishing first-time or one-of-a-kind activities, people can increase their relative productivity by augmenting the process with appropriate tools or resources. If the activities are repetitive and have volume, then work can be automated. Both augmentation and automation improve productivity, but they usually apply to two different extremes of work and use different terminology to describe the benefits. Basically, routine work is measured in terms of efficiency, reactive work is measured in terms of effectiveness, and creative work is measured in terms of innovation.

The benefits of automation are usually evident immediately, but the value of augmentation cannot be measured until tomorrow. Nevertheless, businesses expect principals to conceive, analyze, and formally organize their innovative ideas in some understandable format. Therefore, principals need productivity tools that augment their first-time efforts and increase their effectiveness and ability to be innovative. Managers have been reluctant to help principals augment their creative efforts because they do not know how to justify the augmentation or unpredictable work activities, or put a value on a fuzzy idea. Will the idea, once it is thought through, have value? In order to augment the creative work process, there must be an evaluation system in house. The Work Redistribution Management process (WRM) helps management both manage and justify the cost of an augmentation system. WRM means a new and expanded management process for most businesses. That expanded management process is the heart of this book. In the chapters that follow, we will explore it in all its ramifications, with the overall goal of increased white-collar productivity.

Chapter 2

The Sleeping Giant: Creativity

Corporations face major problems today as they wrestle to stay on top in an increasingly competitive world market. Automation technology has matured; the future will bring appreciable improvements in routine business processes. So the focus now is on increasing white-collar productivity. Yet most executives are in a quandary: Principals either cannot delegate work, or resist delegation, and there is little time or energy left for creative work. Past administrative and clerical support personnel reductions have forced routine tasks back onto the desks of principals, making them increasingly less productive while their challenges grow ever more complex.

Higher white-collar productivity means awakening the brain power that lies dormant in most businesses. In this chapter we consider why principals spend so much time doing routine work. We see how routine work can be delegated through a good support system, and how the way can be cleared to encourage more original thinking and innovative solutions. Lastly, we apply the management principles of Theory X and Theory Y to stimulate the creativity-augmented office of the 1990s.

Routine Work Comes First

In your organization, who accomplishes routine work? Most people reply that their administrative and clerical support personnel perform these tasks. The obvious next question, then, is: Who accomplishes most creative work in your office? Executives, managers, and professionals? Not exactly. Managers and professionals generate most of the creative work, not the executives. Why not? We will explain in Chapter 3, but first let us consider how much time is spent on creative work itself.

This matter was initially researched in 1979 and reported in 1980, one year before the introduction of personal computers. Table 2-1 shows the results discovered at that time, and again in 1988 when the study was repeated.

Why did the percentage of time principals spend on creative work drop in the past ten years? Didn't automation free up more time for creative work?

Routine work is the mainstream of today's business and most of it is implemented by support personnel. Their efforts have high present value for the company, measured in terms of efficiency. Ideally, principals should spend the majority of their time doing creative work. Likewise, creative

Table 2-1. Percentage of time spent on work by type.

	1980		1988	
	Routine	Creative	Routine	Creative
Support Personnel	90%	10%	93%	7%
Principals	48%	52%	63%	37%

work should have high future value for the company. That is why we pay principals a higher salary. They deliver a low-value return when they spend their time on routine work that could be delegated to support personnel. So:

1. Why do principals spend so much time performing routine work?
2. Why isn't more routine work delegated to support personnel?
3. What is this low-value work costing American business?

Principals are paid to modify existing operations to make them more effective, and to create new applications and activities that ultimately lead to a competitive advantage. Support personnel are paid to be both efficient and effective, while implementing the activities and applications that have been delegated to them. As we explained in Chapter 1, work is dynamic, not static. As it evolves from creative to routine, delegation should take place. Unfortunately, that is an infrequent occurrence.

There appears to be a general resistance on the part of managers and staff professionals to delegate work, even though they frequently complain of wasting time doing work that could be done by support personnel. Meanwhile, only a small percentage of support personnel report that they are doing everything they are capable of doing. In fact, many complain of being bored with their work, of not being challenged, and of not having the opportunity to grow in their job.

Professionals frequently feel themselves trapped into performing routine work because:

- It is more comfortable, since the results are predictable.
- It is easier for their managers to measure.
- It is itemized in their formal performance plan (erroneously).

- Support people are not available to be delegated the work.
- Support people, when assigned, are accessible only to "managers."
- Support personnel do not have adequate tools to support the number of principals they are expected to support.
- Support personnel are not trained, so it is easier and less risky for a principal to just "do it myself."

Of course, there are also principals who resist delegating work because they may not have anything to do! If forced to delegate work, some of these people will sit at their desks waiting for the phone to ring or else walk the halls, listening for someone who might need their assistance to "put out another fire." These people need stroking frequently. They must find something else "to do" to feel "valuable" to the organization. They know that much of creative work is done alone, yet they do not like to work alone! They know that when they start a creative process, the results are unpredictable. That uncertainty is stressful and they feel out of control.

The Sad State of Office Work

In October 1983, Rosabeth Moss Kanter published research entitled "Office Automation and People: A New Dimension," the result of a study for a major computer vendor. Some of the findings appeared later in *Management Review.*[1] The study included data collected from 909 pairs of secretaries and managers who worked together on a daily basis, and another 355 secretaries and 28 managers who were not "paired." Of those interviewed, 60 percent had no typewriters, 71 percent had no electronic memory typewriters, 74 percent had no personal computers, 77 percent did not use electronic mail, 80 percent had no electronic scheduling tools, and 91 percent had no electronic filing tools.

The data were collected over six years ago and, obviously, more people are using those tools today. There were two important observations that are still pertinent. First, many senior managers perceive of office work as routine, and their productivity solution is faster hands, so they attempt to automate the office. Second, management must encourage people to experiment, to test and develop new ways of doing business, to take risks. Management must be willing to delegate more responsibility to staff professionals and support people. It must allow people to innovate, and nurture them with the right organization and the right management philosophy.

In Kanter's study, secretaries were asked whether or not they could take on additional responsibility. Only 5 percent said that they could not. Only 25 percent said they were too busy to take on additional tasks *right now*. Obviously, many secretaries and clerical support people feel their skills can be more wisely used.

Support people also expressed disappointment. Kanter explains that 24 percent wanted more information and did not feel they fit into the project; 34 percent wanted to improve their team relationships; 39 percent wanted better communications with management; 40 percent thought the key to increasing their productivity was better technology and tools.

When managers in the same study answered questions about delegating work, 11 percent thought secretaries had enough responsibility, 17 percent thought more teamwork was needed, and 41 percent thought the key to their own productivity was that secretaries should minimize the number of disruptions. Only 24 percent thought secretaries could and should handle more responsibility. Then 50 percent of the managers contradicted themselves by reporting that they wasted more than 10 percent of their time on activities that could and should be delegated. These activities included: supervision of minor tasks and operations; composing routine correspondence, memos, or reports; and making minor decisions.

Kanter also observed that managers:

1. Do not delegate routine tasks to free up more time for important things, "because they are not sure what the more important things would be!"
2. Do not give more information to their support people on a project because they do not get similar information from their own bosses!
3. Do not give secretaries more opportunity to be part of the team because they have never been part of the team themselves!

Their responses are a sad statement about office work! Nearly everyone is comfortable doing predictable and repetitive work. Unfortunately, that is not the reason managers and professionals are paid much higher salaries. Creative work is challenging but it can also be very frustrating, especially if the people, equipment, or procedures in an office do not support it properly.

The Three Components of a Support System

Different types of work demand different support systems, but all share a common characteristic. Every support system has three components: people, equipment, and procedures (PEP) (see Figure 2-1). All business activity can be

Figure 2-1. The PEP triangle.

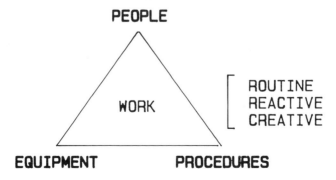

broken down into the three types of work (routine, reactive, and creative), and there should be three different but complementary support systems. As a principal's work changes from creative to routine, it should be delegated to support personnel. The first time a support person performs newly delegated work, it is usually a creative experience, but, when this work also becomes routine for the support person, it should be further delegated to word and data processing systems if there is sufficient volume. If work is routine but low volume, it should be performed by the lowest paid individual in the company who can accomplish it with an augmented system.

Remember:

- When accomplishing routine work, all people generally work the same.
- When accomplishing creative work, all people generally go through similar steps.

However,

- All people do work differently when accomplishing routine work than when accomplishing creative work.

This critical point is not clearly understood, considering current organizational structures and present methods of increasing white-collar productivity. Current organizational structures recognize that all people accomplish routine work in the same way, but there is an underlying assumption reflected in the existing support systems that all work accomplished in an office is the same. Likewise, information technology vendors do not understand that a totally different marketing, justification, implementation, and training approach is needed to meet augmentation needs. Marketing augmentation is not the same as marketing automation.

Subconsciously, most managers know that there are different types of work, requiring different people with different skills. But since management cannot articulate these differences, and because they do not understand that we perform creative work differently, they do not know how to establish a common support system for work, nor do they know how to organize, implement, or justify such a support system. *That is exactly the major problem* in trying to increase white-collar productivity.

We discuss a new justification approach later in this book, but a support system for creative work cannot be implemented without understanding the difference between routine and creative work. To better understand the human limitations we all have that cause us to work differently, see Appendix A.

Technology Can Enhance Creativity

In 1980, approximately 2.7 million U.S. businesses employed administrative and clerical support personnel; that number will increase to 3 million by 1990. Table 2-2 shows the distribution of support personnel in businesses that have an office environment.

When the personal computer was introduced, small companies with fewer than three support people could now afford a computer to accomplish their essential business applications: order entry, billing, inventory control, accounts receivable, sales analysis, general ledger, accounts payable, and payroll. Though a $5,000 to $10,000 computer was a major expense for these small companies, today between 85 and 90 percent have a personal computer.

Companies with four or more support people employ 75 percent of all office employees, and most of these businesses also have a large mainframe computer and a word processing center. So the sales opportunity for initial uses of business computers in America has fairly well matured. The data processing industry now depends on companies to upgrade to larger and larger mainframe computers as they increase the number of activities and applications.

The 40 million white-collar workers in offices today are using between ten and twelve million personal computers,

Table 2-2. Support personnel in establishments with an office environment.

	ESTABLISHMENTS BY THE NUMBER OF SUPPORT PRESENT		
	1-3	4-40	41+
ESTABLISHMENTS (2.7 MILLION)	80%	19%	1%

	PERCENT OF EMPLOYEES IN THESE ESTABLISHMENTS		
SUPPORT (16 MILLION)	25%	38%	37%
PRINCIPALS (24 MILLION)	23%	38%	39%

according to reports in personal computer publications. That is an interesting proportion: Most executives tell us that when 20 to 30 percent of their white-collar workers have a personal computer, the company's need for such devices has matured. The current number of personal computers in use and most executives' intuition of personal computer maturity appear to be the same.

This is an intriguing phenomenon. Computer mainframe manufacturers have a mature business; future computers will be purchased to upgrade systems. On the other hand, computer users have a three- to five-year backlog of new applications they say they want to automate. The manufacturers and users have a complementary need. When manufacturers realize that there are two types of end users— those doing routine work and those doing creative work— perhaps everyone will benefit.

Here is an example to illustrate the point. Computer power is frequently rated in Millions of Instructions per Second, or MIPS. The smaller mainframe computers are three to five MIPS and getting larger. Our experience has shown that, when a work group of 26 end users are integrated with each other and with the mainframe, it increases the MIPS utilization significantly. Since 38 percent of the 40 million end users are employed in 513,000 businesses, and an additional 38 percent are employed in 27,000 businesses, computer companies have a positive growth outlook if they can successfully integrate the end users with the mainframe. But not all users are paid to perform routine work! Businesses must unlock the creative potential of their employees and sort the data processing backlog into creative versus routine activities.

Both manufacturers and users must realize that the computer opportunity is quite mature for routine applications, yet it is very immature for creative solutions. Computer companies have an opportunity to rejuvenate their marketing for both expanded use of mainframe computers and new uses of personal computers. Can the cost of personal computers be justified above the 20–30 percent penetration level? Yes! First we must understand the concepts that support the investment in technology to support creative work, then in Chapter 4 we will see how the concepts develop into reality.

The Detrimental Effect of Automation

To illustrate a point, let us treat all people in the United States as if they worked in one large office. First step back to 1980, and see what the business environment was like. In 1980—the era immediately preceding the introduction of the personal computer—there were 33 million office workers in the United States. Figure 2-2 shows the distribution of principals and support personnel, along with average salaries and the annual total people expense of office work. When

Figure 2-2. 1980 profile of office workers and salary expenses.

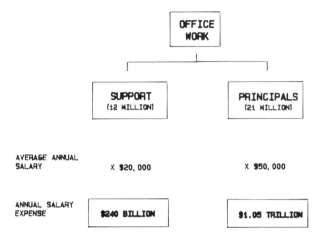

Figure 2-3. 1980 distribution of work and resultant costs.

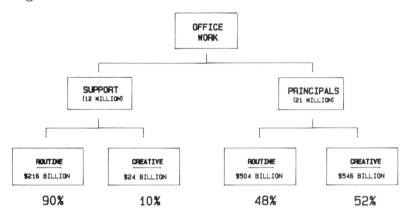

you look at who was doing routine work and who was doing creative work (see Figure 2-3), it is easy to understand why data processing automation and word processing technology were so appealing.

In the majority of analyses we conducted, the 1980 scenario had support personnel performing routine work manually. ("Manually" is defined as using paper and pencil, a calculator, and/or a typewriter or a manual posting procedure.) The computer could handle this routine, repetitive work faster and more accurately whenever there was sufficient volume present to justify the cost of automation. When the volume was present, a computer was purchased, replacing the majority of support personnel previously performing those activities, or else automation was justified by not hiring more support personnel as volume increased.

Unfortunately, this reduction in personnel was done under the assumption that all work in the office is routine. As discussed in Chapter 1, this is not true.

The reduction in support people forced two key things to happen:

1. Low-volume routine work previously performed by support personnel was forced back onto principals to perform. The result? Lower principal productivity.
2. Creative work that naturally evolved into routine work could no longer be delegated, since necessary support people no longer existed. The result? Lower principal creativity.

It is time to turn this situation around and increase white-collar productivity at the same time. It will require a new management approach, a new way of viewing work and of structuring an organization.

Delegate the Routine Work

In 1980, 48 percent of a principal's day was spent on routine work. Follow-up studies in 1988 revealed that the amount of routine work had increased to 63 percent of a principal's day! See Figures 2-4 and 2-5 for the survey results. The price tag for having principals perform routine work had grown to $756 billion annually.

Our studies revealed that up to 70 percent of a principal's routine work could be delegated to support personnel—

Figure 2-4. 1988 profile of office workers and salary expenses.

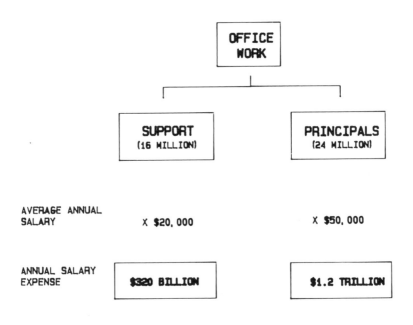

Figure 2-5. 1988 distribution of work and resultant costs.

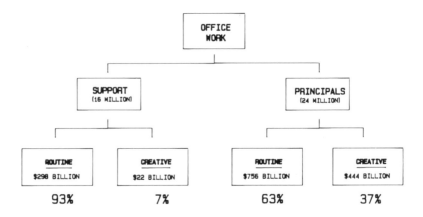

if the support personnel were available. Isn't it better for a $50,000 a year principal to delegate routine work to a $20,000 a year support person? Assume, for the sake of our example, that all office workers actually work in one business environment. Using 1988 figures, 15.1 million principals could be eliminated if *all* their work were delegated to support personnel:

24 million principals × 63% = 15.1 million principals
performing routine work

If only *70 percent* of their routine work could be delegated, 10.5 million could be eliminated:

15.1 million principals × 70% of the routine work that can be delegated = 10.5 million principals

If the business were to hire 10.5 million support people at $20,000 per year, there would be a $315 billion saving every year. (Note that we are *not* encouraging the reduction of principals; we are suggesting that there are better ways to achieve competitive innovation by leveraging the creative efforts of principals! This is demonstrated in Part II, the seven case studies).

10.5 million principals × $50,000/year	= $525 billion
10.5 million support personnel × $20,000/year	= 210 billion
	$315 billion

The question most business leaders ask is: Should I hire more support people and fire my principals? This is the same faulty logic that got companies into trouble with automation. The answer is no—*if* your company depends upon creative work. For example, are you constantly pressured to remain competitive? Do you want to increase sales? In most companies, the day-to-day competitive pressures and the desire to improve mean that sales are dependent upon

creative efforts. When *any* department's success needs creative ideas, you do not want to decrease principal headcount.

In Part II, case studies of various businesses show that
office work and white-collar productivity are not static. As a
company enhances its use of augmentation tools and when
principals can delegate routine work to support personnel,
productivity will increase significantly.

Put Creative Minds to Work

America's next competitive advantage will come from
leveraging its creative brain power, not faster or cheaper
hands. Unfortunately, our culture places more corporate
value on doing than on creating. We are "doers" who measure ourselves against a yardstick of efficiency.

The past reductions in support personnel have made
principals increasingly less productive, yet their challenges
have become more complex. That problem increases geo-
metrically over time. In fact, a professional's job responsibilities have been subtly redefined over the past 30 years. If you
do not believe this has happened in your organization, review
performance plans and then identify which responsibilities
are creative and which are routine!

A number of problems have evolved, including:

1. A lack of support personnel to justify further automation
2. A lack of support personnel to whom future routine
   work can be delegated
3. Resistance on the part of principals to delegate work,
   because "it is easier to do myself" or "it's just part of
   my job now"

The alarming decrease in time spent on creative work
was shown earlier in Table 2-1. Creative work dropped from
constituting 52 percent of a principal's day in 1980 to only
37 percent in 1988!

The first way to leverage principal productivity is to delegate routine work to support personnel. The second way is to increase the time principals actually spend on creative work and to augment their activities. In 1988, the $444 billion spent on creative work could have been far more productive if it had been properly augmented with integrated support tools.

Theory Y and Creative Potential

The notion that all work is routine is the basis for the business philosophy introduced by Douglas McGregor, called Theory X:[2]

> Theory X is the philosophical point of view which states that people are basically lazy and need to be prodded and forced to give a fair day's work for a fair day's wage. People must be managed, monitored and measured closely to ensure that a full day's work is achieved.

McGregor goes on to say that there is another philosophy about work which he called Theory Y. This theory involves:

- Creating opportunities
- Removing obstacles
- Encouraging growth
- Providing guidance

We feel that it is just as natural for a human being to seek creative self-fulfillment on the job as off the job. All management has to do is provide an environment that encourages the employee to pursue an activity on the job which fulfills the employee's perceived needs.

McGregor's theories give us a series of propositions about work, people, and management.

Theory X—Management's Role According to McGregor

1. Management is responsible for organizing elements such as money, materials, equipment, and people for the best economic ends.
2. Management is responsible for directing the efforts of people, motivating them, controlling their actions, and modifying their behavior to fit the needs of the organization.
3. Without active intervention by management, people will be passive, even resistant, to organizational needs. They must, therefore, be persuaded, rewarded, punished, and controlled; their activities must be directed by management. Management gets things done *through* other people.

McGregor explains that Theory X relies on the perception that the average employee:

- Is by nature indolent and works as little as possible; he or she lacks ambition, dislikes responsibility, prefers to be led.
- Is inherently self-centered, indifferent to organizational needs.
- Is by nature resistant to change.
- Is gullible, not very bright, "the ready dupe of the charlatan and the demagogue."

All of us know of some managers who manifest these beliefs, consciously or unconsciously. Now let us look at Theory Y.

Theory Y—Management's Role According to McGregor

1. Management is responsible for organizing elements such as money, materials, equipment, and people for the best economic ends.
2. People are *not* by nature passive or resistant to orga-

nizational needs; they have become so as a result of experience in organizations.

3. The motivation, potential for development, capacity for assuming responsibility, readiness to direct behavior toward organizational goals are all present in people; it is the responsibility of management to make it possible for people to recognize and help individuals develop these characteristics for themselves.

4. The essential challenge of management is to arrange operations so that people can achieve their own goals by directing their own efforts toward organizational goals.

Theory Y managers create *opportunities* for employees to release their potential, while they remove obstacles, manage growth, and provide guidance. This is what Peter Drucker has called Management by Objective.

These philosophies reflect people's attitudes toward business. The attitudes of people are a reflection of management's philosophy. That is why the proper management style is so important to productivity. For example, routine work exists in every business. In some, it is managed with a Theory X style; in others, it is approached with an emphasis on the value of people. We refer to the latter style as Benevolent Theory X management.

Maslow's Hierarchy of Needs

Abraham Maslow's work complements Theories X and Y, and our discussion of work.[3] He classifies the five needs we all have:

1. Physiological—rest, shelter, food, fresh air
2. Safety—protection against danger, threat, or deprivation

3. Social—belonging, giving and receiving friendship and love
4. Ego—self-esteem, self-confidence, independence, achievement, recognition, appreciation
5. Self-fulfillment—self-actualization, self-development

These needs govern our behavior and attitudes, at home and at work. Therefore, a person can just as likely fulfill these needs at work as at home. The extent to which they can be fulfilled at work is largely up to management.

The five needs are in a hierarchical order. If a level of need is satisfied, it is not a motivator of behavior. If it is unsatisfied, it is the current motivator of human behavior. Any needs beyond that level must wait until the current need has been satisfied. Only then will the new need become the motivator.

Maslow noted that the highest level of need—self-fulfillment—is the only one that seems to *increase* as it is gratified, because it is the process of growth. He went on to describe some characteristics of individuals who manifest such needs:

1. Increase in spontaneity
2. Increase in problem-centering
3. Increase in detachment and desire for privacy
4. Increase in autonomy and resistance to following the masses
5. More democratic character structure
6. Greatly increased creativeness

We should point out that Maslow recognized two other needs that transcend the hierarchy: cognitive and aesthetic. Respectively, these refer to one's need to understand the environment and to realize and include beauty and harmony in nature. Cognitive needs are voiced by employees who demand more challenging jobs and want to understand how they fit into the overall design.

With better understanding, managers can begin to see a correlation between Theories X and Y and Maslow's hierarchy of needs. Because management has not understood some of these elements in the office environment, it has focused mainly on the work of support personnel, not principals. For example, we feel that the behavior, attitude, and performance of most individuals working in clerical and administrative support functions are affected by the same needs as those of principals. The attitude and performance of most principals are affected by the degree to which their self-esteem and self-actualization needs are met.

If support people demonstrate frustration with their jobs, it could very well be because management has not recognized their need for self-esteem, achievement, status, and more respect from others. In other words, support personnel are frustrated because they are not being given the opportunity to fulfill their ego and self-fulfillment needs with more challenging creative work.

The opposite may be true for some principals. Some principals were hired to perform creative work, but they just cannot seem to do it! They are not motivated by ego and self-fulfillment, and so they procrastinate creative tasks by surrounding themselves with stacks of routine work. Because such individuals always appear busy, management gives them a free ride, reducing morale among the remaining principals.

Another critical observation is that most managers generally are best suited to manage either routine or creative task-oriented functions and people but not both. Many executives express the view that "managing people is managing people!" If you believe that all people are the same, that all work challenges are the same, and that all managers are the same, then that is absolutely true. Actually, managers' abilities to recognize and empathize with different levels of needs are restricted by their own level of needs.

At first and second levels of management, many managers become frustrated trying to manage "creative professionals." They want to fit everything into neat cubicles of work effort, over-managing every detail to make sure it is progressing on a comfortable path of time and resources, ensuring that everyone is "busy" with something, and insisting on some form of measurement as proof of valuable effort. These are the managers who want lots of meetings, who need to be "kept informed" on a regular basis, who become frustrated when people appear to be "just reading or thinking." These authoritarians are perfect managers for routine work, not creative.

Creative managers are *coaches*. They are not insecure about not appearing to be in control. They understand the creative process and are not frustrated with the absence of measurements and standards. They are listeners who not only are open to off-the-wall ideas but encourage them! They treat employees as peers with valuable ideas and experience. These types usually become higher level executives.

Creative Management in Action

How does all this theory translate into real experience? Let us examine what happened in a sales organization with 21 salespeople. Before implementation of Theory Y management, the average salesperson was 78 percent of the annual quota, and the excellent performer was 115 percent of quota.

Utilizing the management process described in Chapter 7, over a period of a year, the company identified tasks that could be delegated to support personnel. Six additional support people were hired, and the routine activities and applications were delegated. These decisions were made even though there was no authorized headcount from headquarters to hire more support personnel. The move freed up 30 percent of the average sales representative's time!

If asked how much one could expect in incremental sales time from each salesperson, most people would have estimated 20 or 25 percent. As it turned out, 45 percent greater productivity was achieved. Why? If you practice Theory Y, you believe that, when properly supported, principals perform to a higher level than generally expected, that employees will aggressively aspire to the ultimate challenge for their own self-fulfillment. It will be no secret, after reading this book, that we are both strong advocates of Theory Y.

Let us consider these critical questions:

1. When principals delegate routine work to support personnel, shouldn't the number of principals be decreased?
2. Is it possible to determine, before the fact, who to terminate?

After the sales organization mentioned earlier implemented its changes, the range of performance in this local sales office for the 21 sales representatives was 97 percent of quota for the two lowest performers and 368 percent for the highest performer! The *national* average for all sales personnel in the organization was 52 percent of quota halfway through the year. But it was possible for management to identify the two low performers and the two or three high performers before these changes. Suppose a premature attempt had been made to release the two low performers. Consider the performance the company would have missed: These two "low performers" were 45 percent above the national average! This is the main problem with the concept of downsizing. Even though you can now identify the lowest performers, you do not have any idea what type of performance will be achieved when they are supported properly.

What if the sales organization prematurely terminated the five lowest salespeople? How would the company have identified which three additional sales representatives should go? It is much more difficult to identify and accurately rank the three next lowest performers. More important, look at the potential revenue the company would have missed in using the terminations to justify the cost of additional support personnel.

Obviously, the problem is one of accurately predicting people's use of their creative abilities. Sometimes, productivity through creativity comes from unexpected sources. In addition, the redistribution of work, a better support structure, and the resulting productivity gains occurred within 15 months of the start dates. What Theory Y management advocate would not be willing to experiment for 15 months?

There is another aspect of management that comes into play here. It is important to understand that the measurement of productivity is subtle. In the previous sales example, "quota" was easy to establish as the primary factor for measurement. The sales representatives were under the impression that their time was freed up to allow them to concentrate on more creative work—specifically, to meet their customers' needs. The shift in workload put greater responsibility on the sales representatives.

In work groups or departments that do not generate revenue, measurement of productivity may not be as obvious, but it is just as necessary. The key is to look for an increase in the work group's productivity and keep the spotlight off the individual results. The emphasis is on helping management off-load non-productive activities; the productivity increases will come automatically. Productivity measurements are covered in more detail in Chapter 8.

The Challenge of White-Collar Productivity

As an executive of a corporation, where would you rather have a 20 percent productivity improvement?

- In the work of support personnel?
- In the work of principals?

On the basis of the average salaries of 40 million U.S. office workers, a 20 percent increase in the productivity of support personnel would yield a return on investment (ROI) of just over 2 percent. A 20 percent productivity increase in the work of principals would yield an ROI of just over 15 percent. If the answer is so obvious, why have American businesses ignored this opportunity?

The remainder of this book will tackle that question. It will describe how you must get the right work to the right employees. This is not a one-time task, but a continuous fine-tuning process. To accomplish this objective, managers must reevaluate work and the people, procedures, and equipment used. A definition of the "right work" must begin with a clear understanding of the strategic business plan, must include critical success factors, and must focus on the company's products, customers, services, and delivery mechanisms for the next three to five years.

This evaluation means executive involvement to better understand the nature of creative work, how resources can be leveraged, and how the organization can be restructured and fine-tuned as business strategies, people skills, competitive forces, and work challenges change. Anything less is simply throwing technology at a still misunderstood productivity problem. The answer is not just technology.

Chapter 3

Getting the Right Work to the Right People

The fine-tuning of people, equipment, and procedures in an office is an ongoing process. It is the basic work of management. It should *not* be an equipment or software vendor's sponsored one-time study to justify the cost of adding more technology. Rather, management continuously needs to ensure that the "right" office work is performed in the "right" way by the "right" people. In this chapter, we review the way work is distributed and filtered through the traditional organizational structure, and we explain why this method does not work in today's office. You will find nine critical steps to fine-tune the utilization of resources for accomplishing office work, as well as some cautions on people's resistance to change. Our main goal in this chapter is to lay the foundation for our Work Redistribution Management—a systematic means of ensuring that people do the type of work they are paid to do.

High-Value Work

It is a basic objective of business to operate as profitably as it can. Efficiency, effectiveness, and innovation are hallmarks of that profitability. In today's lean-running businesses, human resources must be utilized to their maximum. It is essential that managers fine-tune their office operations. Tied to the strategic business plan, a solid work analysis is the essential tool for redesigning the traditional, bureaucratic corporate structure. World competition demands that businesses of the future be a trim, spider-web network of efficient work groups that enhance the creative process.

Figure 3-1 represents a new organizational design. The concept is simple: To maximize efficiency, effectiveness, and innovation, employees should spend the majority of their time doing the work for which they were *hired*. Principals are hired to perform creative work and support personnel are hired to accomplish routine work. Employees identify with

Figure 3-1. The new organizational design.

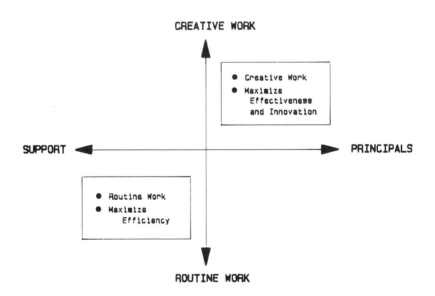

the two basic types of work, and different employees find personal satisfaction in each.

People are paid different compensation because their skills have different potential value to the company. The greater the perceived value, the higher the compensation. Figure 3-2 is a job satisfaction quadrangle that illustrates this point. Optimum satisfaction is in opposing corners for principals and support personnel. This goes back to the personal needs we mentioned in Chapter 2—Abraham Maslow's hierarchy of needs—and it helps us understand people and their relative work desires.

For example, consider support people performing creative work (cell 4) or tasks consistently higher than what they were hired to perform. An apparent benefit to the company is low cost. While such employees may initially welcome such challenging work as a temporary relief from repetitive work, it is only a short time before those "unrecognized, unrewarded" individuals feel the company is taking advantage of them—that is, giving low pay for a high-skilled activity or greater responsibility. Likewise, consider a principal spend-

Figure 3-2. The job satisfaction quadrangle.

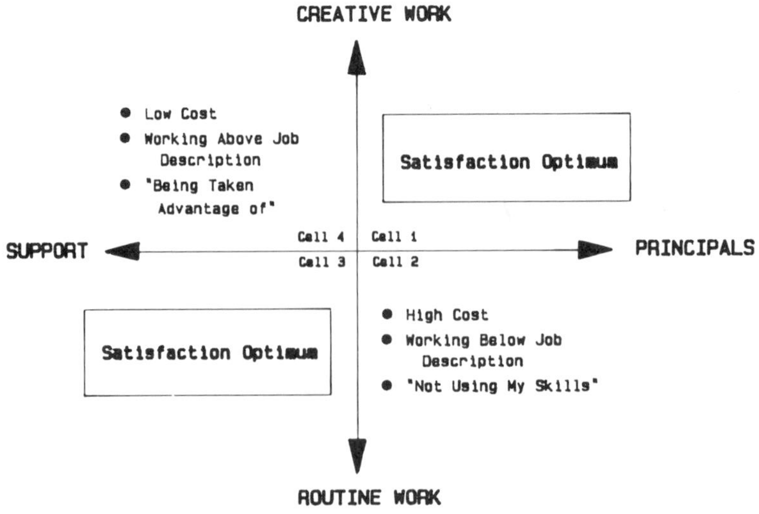

ing time on routine work (cell 2). This is low-value work for the company and it often leads to poor morale and performance malaise.

Principals and support people are *not* equivalent resources. "That is obvious!" you exclaim. Then why do companies continue to confuse the two? The decision as to which person should perform which job is a costly one if not made with understanding. How does management ensure that the right work gets to the right people? With a plan for how work should be distributed and managed.

Creative Work and Myopic Management

In Chapter 2, we asked who spends the majority of time on the creative work—executives, managers, or staff professionals? Many people would have responded "top executives." They are paid the most, but this is not exactly correct. While it may be true that top executives are very creative, they use their "creative" skills evaluating the creative work done by others. Creative work is usually done by staff professionals (step 1 in Figure 3-3). The creative work is then presented to a manager and evaluated (step 2 in Figure 3-3). The manager decides to modify, continue, cancel, approve, or forward the creative work to top management (step 3 in Figure 3-3). The executive then either rejects, modifies, or accepts the creative work.

When the creative work is accepted by management, a major error is often made. The staff professional who initially performed the creative work is made responsible for implementing the recommendations (step 4 in Figure 3-3). This is acceptable as an *initial* approach, but causes problems later on. We are all not equally endowed with creative ability, and a company must use this resource wisely. The skills required to implement the recommendations must be identified quickly and then the responsibility transferred, releasing the creative person to work on other high-value projects.

Another mistake is often made at the point where cre-

Figure 3-3. The delegation of work as it dynamically changes from creative to routine.

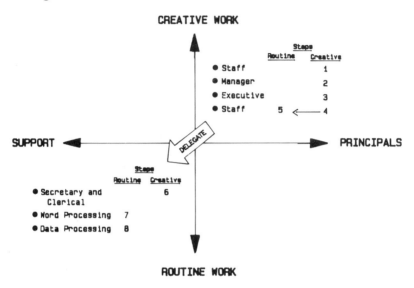

ative work is transferred. The work is delegated from the creative staff originator to another staff professional (step 5 in Figure 3-3). At first, the work is creative, but over time it becomes routine. As soon as possible, that routine task should be delegated to a support person (step 6 in Figure 3-3). At this point it can be a challenging, creative experience that adds to the support person's sense of worth to the company. Normally, this delegation does not occur, in spite of the overwhelming logic that it is better to have a $20,000 resource perform the work instead of a $50,000 person. But if such delegation to support personnel does occur, over time it will also become routine for them. If this delegated work then increases in volume, either word processing or data processing (automation) should be used to make the process more efficient (steps 7 and 8 in Figure 3-3).

By the time this work is delegated to a support person, it is extremely obvious that the work has become routine. Too frequently, only the obvious activities and applications— those characterized by volume and frequency—are delegated. As a result, technology vendors approach a business with a vast array of solutions that are faster and more efficient. In the majority of cases, this "volume work solution" mentality results in the data processing and word processing technology investments of today's business world.

This myopic view of work and office support systems has led to two critical misconceptions about office work:

1. All work performed in an office is routine.
2. Only predictable, high-volume, repetitious work can benefit from automation or an office support system.

A New Division of Labor

A redesigned organizational structure encourages maximum utilization of resources, both human and technological. To reach that goal, there are nine key steps:

1. Understand the company's strategic business objectives.
2. Break down the strategic business objectives into the lowest business function possible and identify which functions have the greatest impact on the strategic objective.
3. Identify which work groups have the greatest contribution to each respective business function. Then prioritize the work groups by the critical nature of their contribution, that is, by their ability to address critical success factors.
4. Identify routine work performed by principals and also that performed by support personnel within the work groups.
5. Delegate routine work to support personnel.
6. Increase or change the support structure to absorb incremental routine work. Increase the number of people or the amount of equipment.

7. Identify and prioritize the creative needs of the business.
8. Augment the work of principals and support personnel with tools that assist in their reactive and creative work.
9. Evaluate the expense and benefit of increased high-value work.

Note that it is not enough just to spend more time on creative, high-value work. In Chapter 7, we detail a well-defined process to continuously identify, evaluate, and document the benefits of creative work. Work Redistribution Management (WRM) is a methodology to analyze routine, reactive, and creative activities, and it can be used to restructure an organization's support system to ensure that the right work is accomplished by the right people. A side benefit is that the process can also be used to measure the benefits of investments in office technology. It can help document the use of personal computers, problem-solving tools, corporate databases, and communications systems between employees and suppliers, distributors, and other external partnerships.

The Best Person for the Job

The first move toward greater efficiency and productivity is to identify the routine activities and applications that principals are performing that could be shifted to support personnel. As mentioned in Chapter 2, our studies indicate that approximately 70 percent of the routine work of principals can be delegated (see Figure 3-4). Of course, certain work occurs too infrequently to delegate, for example, filling out a time card once a week. Use the general rule of thumb: When the time it takes to delegate the activity is equal to or greater than the time it takes to do it yourself, do it yourself. However, be careful! Do not use this as a rationale to resist delegating on a continuous basis.

Figure 3-4. The routine work to delegate.

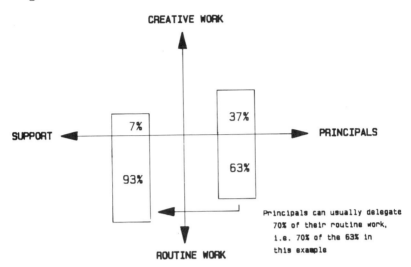

Of course, if management wants to delegate work but it does not have the support structure—that is, the people, equipment, and procedures (PEP)—in place today, what are the options? It may be easier and less costly just to continue the current mode of operation, but do not expect to stay competitive. Likewise, management cannot justify the cost of bolstering one corner of the PEP support triangle by chipping away at another corner.

Today's common technology justification is: Reduce support personnel to pay for data and word processing automation. Businesses continue to treat investments for creative-work support systems the same as those to automate routine tasks. Instead, businesses should measure the cost of an improved support system against the increased revenue generated or saved through the support of creative work. This is a new perspective for measuring performance as well.

The answer to increased white-collar productivity is not only better tools for leveraging brain power and teamwork, but better management. Better management begins with gathering information. As managers review the performance plans and job descriptions of their employees, they need to ask themselves why they are paying principals to perform routine work, and why they are not challenging support people with more responsibility.

Such challenges can nurture loyalty. Everyone needs to grow. If managers do not identify and implement the right support system for each type of work, then they should be replaced because that is essential to good management. Even heavy routine work can be made more enjoyable if management is receptive to worker ideas on modifying existing procedures. When such modifications are suggested, managers should encourage support personnel and provide incentives for them to make the modifications themselves.

For example, let us assume that you are a principal and have created a weekly report on your personal computer, using graphics and a spreadsheet. Over time, the report has become predictable and routinized, so you delegate it to a clerical person who has a personal computer with the same hardware and software. One day the clerical person comes to you with an idea for improving the spreadsheet analysis and new ideas for better graphics in the reports.

If the clerical job is narrowly defined, and there has been little training for the support person on spreadsheet and graphics software, you may accept the idea, interrupt a current work effort, and make the changes. If months have passed since the original delegation, however, you probably have become involved in another project and such changes are a low priority. In fact, you may not remember the details of that spreadsheet and graphics application and may simply ignore the request for enhancements.

What if the clerical person were trained on the software, and not only were given an opportunity to make the enhancements (after you reviewed them) but had his or her job description expanded to include identifying such improvements and performing the modifications? The result would be a win-win situation: The employee wins and the business wins.

Change and the RC Factor

A new management outlook implies change, a major change in philosophy, in the distribution of work, in the measurement of productivity. Management must be dynamic and willing to change in order to get the right job to the right employee. Likewise, employees must be willing to change in order to better perform the jobs they are paid to perform.

When attempting to manage change in the office environment, managers must be sensitive to the resistance to change that is inherent in the human condition. We call this resistance the RC Factor, and a better understanding of it will help smooth the way to an effective redistribution of work.

We all resist changes that transform our comfort level in terms of the work we perform and our individual work habits. It takes time to acclimate to change. There is a learning curve, which traces the pattern of initial resistance to final acceptance. For instance, productivity dips temporarily during the learning process. The depth and length of the dip varies, depending upon the quantity and extensiveness of the modifications or innovations.

The productivity dip is also affected by a sensitivity to change itself. If the people being asked to change perceive an insensitive management, the dip in productivity is deeper and more extended. Typically, these same insensitive managers also miss the fact that productivity is lagging until it becomes a crisis. However, if those requested to implement changes perceive a sensitive management, they usually lower their resistance and accept and implement the desired changes. The result is a more shallow and shortened productivity dip. This is how the RC Factor works.

Let us use a simple experiment to see the RC Factor in action. Working with a small group of people, ask: "Which is faster, writing a six-letter word or a twelve-letter word?" Most people will opt for the logical answer of six. Now ask them to repeatedly write the twelve-letter word "improvements." After one minute, stop them and determine the average number of times each person wrote the word.

Now tell the audience that when you say go, they will have one minute to write the six-letter word that is made up of every other letter in the word "improvements," starting with the letter i, then immediately say go. Do not acknowledge or answer any questions until the time is up. People will be frustrated. They will raise their hands, mumble to each other, and stammer (resistance to change). Finally, once they realize you are ignoring them and concentrating on the time, they will grudgingly start.

What happened? First, you asked them to do something new, something they had not done before, something creative. They had never written the word "ipoeet." It was creative to ascertain what was to be written, but was it a word? "No!" is their response. "This isn't fair! This is not a word! Maybe I misunderstood! Should I really do this? This does not feel right!" Ask them to count the number of times they wrote "ipoeet" (more mumbling and moaning), then record the average. It should be roughly the same for the six letters as for the twelve letters they used when writing the word "improvements"—that is, no productivity increase and they only accomplished half the work.

Now acknowledge that you asked the group to write a "questionable" word that does not exist in the English language. Tell them that their reaction was normal, and compliment them on their ability to decipher your short instructions and their general performance and cooperation. Now ask them again to write the word "ipoeet" for one more minute. Compare the results. Obviously, after a demonstration of your sensitivity, the general resistance to change was overcome and the productivity is where you would expect it, about double that of writing a twelve-letter word.

Once again, tell them that when you say go, they will have one minute to write the six-letter "word" that is made up of every other letter in the word "acknowledges," starting with the letter *a*, then immediately say go. This time, you will see more cooperation. Determine the average number of times the word "akolde" has been written and compare the results. You should find a different productivity this time as a result of reducing the resistance to change.

This experiment shows how the RC Factor was lowered. First, the word "akolde" was different and new, but the work process was not. Second, the audience knew that you empathized with the problem, that you were not trying to make them look dull or stupid, that you made it a team challenge! Management that wants to decrease resistance to change should show its sensitivity to the difficulties of the change process and make change itself a team effort.

Work Redistribution Management

We began this chapter by suggesting a new organizational design. Our Work Redistribution Management (WRM) process is the basis for implementing that design, one that encompasses a redefinition of work performed in the office. We will explain more about this process in Chapter 7, but for now let us examine how it complements the new organizational design.

Work Redistribution Management answers the following questions:

- How do you identify work to be delegated?
- How do you identify the new creative work to be accomplished by principals?
- How do you measure the benefits of this new creative work?
- How do you augment the principal's productivity?

We agree with the words of D. F. (Scott) Sink, director of the Virginia Productivity Center: "You cannot manage what you cannot measure. You cannot measure what you cannot define. You cannot define what you do not understand." In

Chapter 1, we gave the definitions that underlie this process, specific meanings for such generally used words as "office," "work," and "automation." We also described the types of work, to better identify what can be delegated and what is considered creative. WRM provides the means of identifying different types of work in the office and measuring output.

In an engineering firm, a second-level manager had the responsibility to produce a procedure manual for nuclear plants. He could not do so because each week he had to call the various remote sites to prepare payroll. He would get each employee's hours and manually prepare the payroll amounts. During the WRM process, we asked him if he felt he was the right person for that job. He looked at us in astonishment and then laughed. He said, "This sure is a simple process, isn't it?" Many times it is. About 70 percent of the work principals identify as routine can be delegated to support personnel, yet most principals are too close to the trees to see the forest. The WRM process makes the misappropriations of work more obvious.

New activities and applications have their genesis in ideas. Ideas that need time and effort to develop, however, are often smothered by routine work. The Work Redistribution Management process helps identify what creative things need to be done, and helps management set priorities. With 70 percent of their routine work reallocated, principals can devote a higher percentage of their total time to high-value creative activities.

Many articles have been written on proving a productivity increase, but the essential question is whether the activity one is attempting to measure and evaluate has value to the company. The people, time, energy, and cost associated with the production of a product or service is a business's initial standard for productivity. If the product or service sells, the company is a success as long as profits exceed cost. So improvements in products, services, and costs are measured in terms of the value-added activities of the business and specific work-group objectives. WRM documents the activities of work groups so that they can be measured qualitatively in relation to the overall business objectives.

The routine applications of automation have been explored elsewhere; in this book we concentrate on the augmentation tools for creative work, the subject of our next chapter.

Chapter 4
Integrated Support Systems

At this point you are probably wondering when we are going to get down to specifics, to the nuts and bolts of our productivity recommendations. Well, in Chapter 2 we introduced the three components of a support system, our PEP triangle consisting of people, equipment, and procedures. Now we concentrate on the augmentation tools and how people use the tools. This is your company's productivity opportunity worth billions. It is the challenge of integrating people and the types of work they perform, with the resulting promise of greater white-collar productivity.

In this chapter, we explain five basic business functions and who uses them. Further exploration of this idea leads us to a review of the fourteen software tools, or facilities, which together constitute an integrated office software network. In doing so, we show how equipment in today's modern offices can facilitate the natural flow from creative to routine work.

Complementary tools are needed for both principals and support personnel to allow the delegation of work.

The Five Basic Business Functions

Virtually all work activity in an office can be divided into five basic *functions*:

1. Access to Information
2. Problem Solving
3. Document Preparation and Processing
4. Distribution
5. Communication

Table 4-1 shows the average distribution of a principal's daily total time in each of the five business functions.

Table 4-2 shows the average distribution of a principal's daily time in each of the five business functions in terms of how much of the activity is spent on routine versus creative work efforts. (A business process tends to cross functions and encompass multiple activities and applications. Certain

Table 4-1. Average distribution of principal's total time.

	ACCESS TO INFORMATION	PROBLEM SOLVING	DOCUMENT PREPARATION/ PROCESSING	DISTRIBUTION	COMMUNICATION
TOTAL TIME	18%	20%	29%	1%	32%

Table 4-2. Routine vs. creative time spent by principals in business functions.

	ACCESS TO INFORMATION	PROBLEM SOLVING	DOCUMENT PREPARATION/ PROCESSING	DISTRIBUTION	COMMUNICATION
ROUTINE	70%	74%	65%	100%	65%
CREATIVE	30%	26%	35%	–	35%

business functions are associated more frequently with routine or creative work, depending on the person's responsibilities.) It appears from the two tables that the principal spends the majority of total time in Problem Solving, Documentation, and Communications functions and a large percentage of his or her effort on routine activities. This indicates a number of potential delegation possibilities:

1. Routine work that could be delegated
2. Routine work that could be automated
3. Routine and creative work that could be augmented

We have already emphasized that it is not enough simply to spend more time on high-value activities. In order for principals and support personnel to work more efficiently and effectively, they need better training in using certain basic equipment and common software tools, which will subsequently allow them to perform these functions not only faster but also with greater insight.

Can you draft a formal document on your personal computer, send the document to your secretary for editing, and have the secretary send it electronically to the designated personnel in your organization? Can you create a spreadsheet shell for a specific need and then send the shell to other managers and professionals to use on their personal computers?

Most people answer no. Their company either has no business communications strategy or has never set any standards for hardware and software. It is critical that a business establish tight standards for selecting workstations and compatible communications tools. The basis for such standards is compatible equipment as well as compatible software that *all* employees need to support the five basic functions.

The Fourteen Facilities

The software tools are called *facilities*, and they provide the ability to augment as well as automate the work people accomplish while using the fourteen facilities in the five basic functions. Figure 4-1 shows these facilities and the functions of which they are a part. (*Note:* We are including "expert systems" in the facility called "artificial intelligence.")

Most top management, most support personnel, and many staff professionals require only the facilities identified under Documentation, Distribution, and Communication. We call these the *basic work facilities*. The remainder, *data facilities*, are used by office workers who analyze information. The basic work facilities, coupled with data facilities, are referred to as *foundation facilities*. A third category of software tools is called *line-of-business*, or industry, software. There is also a fourth category, infrastructure software, that supports office work. This includes security systems, operating system software, and network management software (we will not discuss this fourth category in this book).

These three levels of software cover all the activities and applications performed by most office workers. Thus, the 40 million office workers in the United States today need intelligent workstations with access to these augmentation facilities.

Figure 4-1. The five functions and fourteen facilities.

ACCESS TO INFORMATION	PROBLEM SOLVING	DOCUMENT PREPARATION/ PROCESSING	DISTRIBUTION	COMMUNICATION
Document Library Services	Spreadsheet	Word Processing	Document Distribution	Telephone Management
Central Data Base Query	Graphics	Notes and Messages	Scanning	Calendar, Meetings, and Scheduling
Data Download	Artificial Intelligence	Imaging		
		Printing and Publishing		

Which Workers Need Which Facilities?

Your first reaction may be that some workers do not require access to a central database or document library services, or that secretaries would rarely use a spreadsheet or graphic capabilities if delivered to them. That may be true *today!* Remember that quick conclusions are often based on wrong assumptions. In this case, recall a point made earlier: Work is dynamic; much of what is creative today will be routine tomorrow.

When work is delegated to the right people, and the right people are accomplishing the right work, all support personnel and all principals should have access to *all* fourteen facilities for the following reasons:

- What people accomplish today is not what they will always be doing. For principals to have the freedom to delegate, all personnel must have quick access to the same facilities. In fact, the role of support personnel will change the quickest.
- Many people require access to corporate, department, or work-group data. If they do not have computer access, reports must be rekeyed into their personal computers.
- The cost of supplying people with intelligent workstations and the accompanying software is minimal when compared to the productivity jump that results.

The basic work facilities will be used by all personnel. Data facilities will initially be used by staff professionals and managers who select, sort, and manipulate data in a problem-solving process. As part of that analysis, they may wish to display, chart, or graph the information and then store it for future reference. To fully leverage their productivity, professional staff and managers need access to existing databases, which are a historical accumulation of "automated" operations.

Assume that you are a financial analyst (professional staff) in a company's business planning department. You are given the challenge to develop a three-year sales forecast by product class, customer set, and geographic segment, and then must compare that with industry-wide projections. The first step in this creative process may be to gather information and verify that you have an accurate list of product classes. Your second step may be to classify customer sets by historical revenue volume, industry classifications, number of employees, and so on. Third, you would probably retrieve sales from the past three to five years by geographic segment, so as to analyze product, customer, and seasonal trends.

If such historical information does not exist as a result of automated business applications, it is very difficult to gather the data. You may have to search multiple archived files in numerous locations. The availability of certain data facilities could tremendously augment your ability to access information and perform a thorough analysis.

These facilities provide a solid foundation so that people can work more effectively and work can easily be redistributed within and between work groups, providing a synergistic approach to accomplishing all office work. Obviously, other software tools such as advanced statistical analysis and sophisticated desktop publishing capabilities are valuable additions to any office. Each set of facilities is essential for sharing of information among all personnel in the organization, yet each has its own scope or sphere of influence.

Line-of-Business Software

The third group of facilities tend to be specialized facilities and are often referred to by three different names: line-of-business, department applications, and industry applications. The most frequent department-controlled applications are payroll, billing accounts payable, accounts receivable, inventory control, general ledger, and order entry.

These are generic applications that transcend virtually every business.

In addition, there are industry-specific applications such as material requirements planning, installment loan accounting, patient admitting, actuarial accounting, computer-aided design, computer-aided manufacturing, and so on. Many of these applications are routine data processing programs that build up databases. Others are creative tools to solve ad hoc business problems, or are specific applications required to help principals in solving problems.

One of the largest problems in the software marketplace is the use of the term "office." "Office software" is a tragic and restrictive misnomer. As we established in Chapter 1, the office is where people work. *All* software used in an office is office software. What vendors are trying to say is that their "office" software (augmentation) tools are different from the fixed-function programs (automation programs). Using their terms, "office" software augments the first-time processing of ideas with a volume of one. Fixed-function software automates repetitive, high-volume applications such as accounts payable, payroll, order entry, and general ledger.

Now that we have our definitions of software, let us look at how different levels of personnel spend their respective time on each of the five basic business functions.

Top Management

Top management is the 720,000 executives who make up roughly 3 percent of the total number of principals and 2 percent of the total office population. How does top management typically distribute its time? Which augmentation facilities can help top management accomplish its job more effectively? See Figure 4-2. Note that this figure, and the similar ones that follow, are overviews only; thus, time expenditures are general, rounded figures, and it is possible to have a time expenditure without a key facility represented or a facility without a significant amount of time expended.

Figure 4-2. Distribution of top management's time and key facilities required.

ACCESS TO INFORMATION	PROBLEM SOLVING	DOCUMENT PREPARATION/ PROCESSING	DISTRIBUTION	COMMUNICATION
II. Data Facilities		I. Basic Work Facilities		

Document Distribution   Telephone Management

Notes and Messages   Calendar, Meetings, and Scheduling

Time Expenditures:

| 12% | 4% | 27% | – | 57% |

What type of work does top management spend the majority of its time performing? The answer is not as apparent as it seems. Top executives spend most of their time communicating—more specifically, by listening and thinking. They evaluate the creative work others have accomplished, presented to them in the form of facts, opinions, ideas, and recommendations. Their response to staff presentations may be one of the following:

"Yes, do it!"
"No, I don't like that idea!"
"Good work, but let's modify the approach."
"Here are some ideas that I want you to explore and get back to me with next month."
"Discontinue work on that immediately."
"Determine the cause of the situation in more detail."
"Continue investigating that idea. When I have more information, I'll schedule time to consider it."

"Creative" executive work is the thinking and evaluation process itself, which is a reaction to an event or information for which the executive must make a judgment. He or she spends most of the day doing reactive-creative and reactive-routine work. Top management decisions direct someone either to do more creative work (reactive-creative) or to execute some predefined routine task (reactive-routine). Executives are paid to listen, evaluate, plan, and make decisions; other principals in the organization are paid to gather and analyze information, to explore innovative and workable solutions, and to implement the executive's decisions.

Management

This level of management is from vice president on down to first-level managers. It constitutes about 6,250,000 people—26 percent of the office principals and 15 percent of the total white-collar population. How does management typically distribute its time? See Figure 4-3. The work management most frequently performs is reactive-creative and reactive-routine.

Remember the three sizes of businesses mentioned earlier? Companies can be grouped as (1) those with one to three support personnel, (2) those with four to forty, and (3) those with forty-one or more support people. Obviously, vice presidents in the largest corporations have hundreds of employees reporting to them. Their workday is very much like a top executive's schedule, with much of the time devoted to listening, evaluating, and making decisions. In medium-size companies, vice presidents may use a hands-on approach. They may spend more time on creative work, performing their own problem-solving tasks and accessing their own information.

For example, a chief financial officer (CFO) of a hospital initially had data loaded to a relational database to accomplish a few high-priority applications that he had thought of initially. While extracting and analyzing the data, the CFO

Figure 4-3. Distribution of management's time and key facilities required.

ACCESS TO INFORMATION	PROBLEM SOLVING	DOCUMENT PREPARATION/ PROCESSING	DISTRIBUTION	COMMUNICATION
II. Data Facilities		I. Basic Work Facilities		
	Spreadsheet	Word Processing	Document Distribution	Telephone Management
	Graphics	Notes and Messages	Scanning	Calendar, Meetings, and Scheduling

Time Expenditures:

| 19% | 10% | 31% | – | 40% |

discovered certain key financial indicators quite by accident. He decided to track these indicators by downloading the variables onto a spreadsheet as each was discovered. Over a nine-month period, he discovered 23 key monthly indicators that clearly showed the financial health of the hospital on a monthly basis.

After tracking the data for months, the CFO used a graphics software package on his personal computer to create an animated presentation complete with colorful charts and diagrams. He explained the importance of the indicators to the board of directors and how his findings were quite accidental, through using some basic augmentation tools he had never been given before. Everyone was impressed and invested in similar tools for other office workers.

Notice in Figure 4-3 that a fair amount of time is spent accessing information. Depending on the size of the business, this may be done by managers themselves or by asking staff professionals and support personnel to gather data. In large companies, the facilities used most frequently by management are similar to those of top management, but there is a little more emphasis on notes and messages, used for informal communications. The time spent in formal communications is mostly a review and sign-off process.

Normally, then, first- and second-level managers do reactive-creative work. In meetings with higher-level management, they are updated on corporate changes, report on progress in meeting objectives, and highlight new situations which must be addressed. The second portion of their meeting time is spent with colleagues and professional staff, where they evaluate ideas and provide continuing direction to personnel who actually roll up their sleeves and accomplish the work.

Professional Staff

This is the largest group of principals, approximately 17 million workers, and it includes salespeople, technical personnel, scientific experts, engineers, and those referred to as professional staff. It does *not* include secretaries or administrative clerical support staff.

These 17 million professionals constitute the largest expense and the greatest potential for creative work. Remember, fewer than 500,000 businesses employ 75 percent of this population. This is where the majority of creative and reactive-creative work normally exists in most organizations. Which facilities do these people use? See Figure 4-4.

Business's dependency on staff professionals to accomplish creative work is somewhat self-evident when you realize that typically 72 percent of their time is spent accessing information, solving problems, and preparing documentation. That is why augmenting the work of staff professionals is so critical to increasing white-collar productivity.

For example, a staff professional has just been hired with the immediate assignment to:

Figure 4-4. Distribution of professional staff's time and key facilities required.

ACCESS TO INFORMATION	PROBLEM SOLVING	DOCUMENT PREPARATION/ PROCESSING	DISTRIBUTION	COMMUNICATION
II. Data Facilities		I. Basic Work Facilities		
Document Library Services	Spreadsheet	Word Processing	Document Distribution	Telephone Management
Central Data Base Query	Graphics	Notes and Messages	Scanning	Calendar, Meetings, and Scheduling
Data Download	Artificial Intelligence	Imaging		
		Printing and Publishing		

Time Expenditures:

19%	24%	29%	–	28%

- Track monthly sales
- Determine the cost of sales
- Calculate the profit
- Analyze the return on investment by product

Done manually, this could be not only time consuming but subject to numerous calculation errors. Once the analysis is performed, the staff person needs to document the results and communicate them. Twenty years ago, the tool for this may have been an adding machine. Ten years ago, it may have been an electronic calculator. Today, it is a personal computer with spreadsheet, graphics, a text editor, and software that can query the corporate database.

Remember that when the original creative activity becomes routine, the volume may be too low to be automated on the mainframe, but it should still be delegated to support personnel. It can be—if they have compatible tools. In this same sense, routine work can also be augmented if the volume is low.

Administrative and Clerical Support Personnel

The last group is the second largest, constituting 16 million people or 40 percent of the office population. Which of the facilities does this group use the majority of the time? See Figure 4-5. As mentioned in Chapter 2, this work is mostly routine or reactive-routine.

In recent years, administrative and support personnel have become very limited in their ability to support principals. This is the traditional group that technology vendors target for personnel reductions to help justify expenditures for automation. As the ranks have been depleted over time, the support work force has done increasing amounts of

Figure 4-5. Distribution of administrative support personnel's time and key facilities required.

ACCESS TO INFORMATION	PROBLEM SOLVING	DOCUMENT PREPARATION/ PROCESSING	DISTRIBUTION	COMMUNICATION
II. Data Facilities		I. Basic Work Facilities		
		Word Processing	Document Distribution	Telephone Management
		Notes and Messages	Scanning	Calendar, Meetings, and Scheduling

Time Expenditures:

15%	3%	59%	11%	12%

routine work. With fewer support personnel on hand, principals also are doing more routine, low-value work.

It is obvious that routine office work must be identified and delegated to support personnel. As this occurs, the job description of the support person is enriched. The following example shows just how fast it can change.

Remember the CFO who presented the 23 key indicators at a hospital board meeting? After the meeting, we asked the president of the hospital if the analysis he had just been presented with was a creative or a routine effort. He replied, "creative." Then we asked the CFO if the previous months' effort was creative or routine. He also said, "creative." You probably have guessed the next question: "Would you like this report monthly?" He replied, "Yes!" We then asked the CFO if next month's report would be creative or routine. He replied, "routine."

Management now had a choice. Both the president and the CFO agreed:

1. That the desired activity and application had repetitive value
2. That the work was now routine and not creative

They were at the pivotal point in the WRM productivity process, which requires a new management philosophy: Who is the right person to accomplish this job? It was obvious that the CFO's time was too valuable. The CFO said, "The comptroller can do it!"

"Do you really want someone at that level to perform a task that is now routine?" they were asked. The CFO quickly responded, "No one else who has a personal computer knows how to use the spreadsheet software and how to access the data."

"So, you are saying that the comptroller, who is paid almost as much as you are, is the right person to do that job because he is the only other person in the department who has the equipment and is trained on the software?"

"Basically."

There was only one more question we wanted the CFO to think about: "What will you do next week, next month, and in the following months when you create similar applications?" They looked at each other. Both quickly agreed that the work should be immediately delegated to a support person. But to whom? We quickly pointed out a couple of facts.

First, this organization, like others in the process of justifying the cost of data and word processing systems, assumed that all work was routine. They had depleted their supply of support people. Second, there are not many support people today who were trained to use a personal computer to:

1. Do a relational database query
2. Run a spreadsheet
3. Utilize a software program that generates presentation graphics

Management decided to expand the current job descriptions, either hire new people or train existing ones in the hospital, and provide more personal computers and the appropriate software. No small effort, but nothing worthwhile is easy or free!

Compatibility Across the Nation

The personal computer is the first major office tool that can help improve principal productivity by augmenting the creative process. At the same time, it can enhance the role of support personnel with more challenging responsibilities. The personal computer is a major step in the information revolution, with the potential to change what we do in the office, who does it, and how it is done. To be successful, businesses need to change their thinking about work, people, and productivity.

For the personal computer to be effective, top management must set a corporate standard for software. That standard must guarantee that the three types of applications—basic work facilities, data facilities, and line-of-business software—be compatible for all workers *within* the corporation as well as with other corporations. Standards must allow the transfer of information through software programs from one employee to another, transparent to the end user. This is *not* a decision for a division, department, or work group. It is a corporate management policy led by the major computer companies in the United States. The personal computer has transformed the computer from an isolated tool to a key part of an integrated information system, like the telephone. Just as you can telephone a friend at the other end of the country, using different phone companies in the process, so too you should be able to access information in data systems in other computer networks. A commonality of software and networks will unite us all in the competitive, fast-paced global market of the 1990s.

The Three Design Components

How does this concept apply to typical office activities? To understand this, you have to examine a workstation and how it should be used. Each of the user workstations in U.S. businesses requires the following capabilities as shown in Figure 4-6. There are three design components required to support the three types of work. The identification process

Figure 4-6. Workstation capabilities.

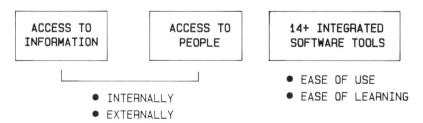

starts with the workstation requirements in various work groups. Once the needs of a work group are understood, up to three integrated design components may be needed.

Fixed-Function Terminals

The first design component supports work that has frequent use and volume. The work flow can be diagrammed, as shown in Figure 4-7.

The solution in this process is usually automation, and the people who do the work are generally support personnel. The programs as well as data are located on the host computer. The job description is very narrow, since the volume does not allow time to perform other work. As a result, fixed-function terminals are used.

Intelligent Workstations

The second major design component involves work with low volume but routine performance. Figure 4-8 shows the work flow.

Figure 4-7. Repetitive high-volume work.

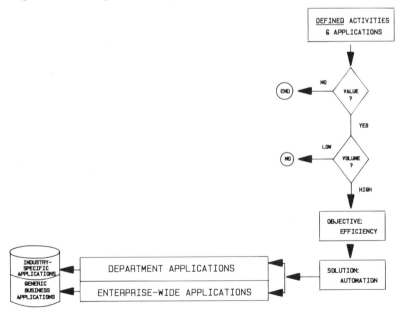

Figure 4-8. Repetitive low-volume work.

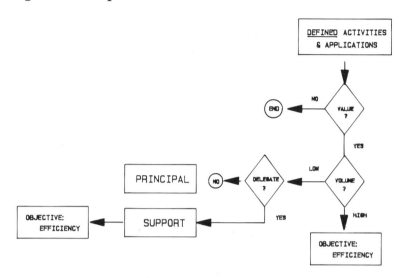

Formal automated data and word processing systems are not the answer. In this case, the work can best be accomplished by one of the group's members using some augmentation tools. Management must ask whether it wants a $50,000 or a $20,000 a year employee to accomplish the work.

In most cases, the answer is the lower paid employee. The work is delegated to a support person, and an *intelligent* workstation is used to make the activities more efficient. The delegation also makes the principal more effective, but compatibility is critical for delegation to be possible.

Creative Augmentation

The third design component is for creative work. It has two aspects; one was shown in Figure 4-8, the other is shown in Figure 4-9. Figure 4-9 addresses work that is defined but has a low or unpredictable volume and is not delegated to administrative or clerical support personnel. Instead the principal retains ownership and performs these activities,

Figure 4-9. Defined, non-delegable, low-volume work.

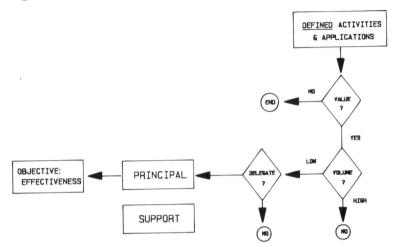

but the objective is to increase the principal's "effectiveness" with augmentation tools.

If the principal requires information to resolve a problem, then the system must allow access to departmental, corporate (and external) databases. In addition, good communications and distribution networks are mandatory.

Figure 4-10 shows the flow for purely creative work that is undefined, non-delegable, and performed by a principal. This is a first-time creative effort, which may start with an idea but the next step is information gathering. Many times the information required already exists in the corporate databases, which are the result of automated applications. The objective in this process is neither effectiveness nor efficiency but innovation—trying to do entirely new things.

The Complete Picture

When we put all three design components together, they appear as shown in Figure 4-11. This integrated system enables you to look at your business in a different light. First,

Figure 4-10. Undefined, non-delegable, low-volume work.

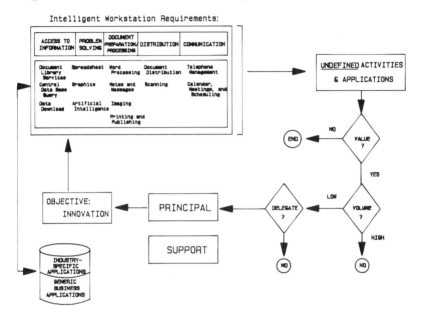

there is a software link between support personnel and principals which allows work to be delegated easily. Second, the different types of work and required support systems suggest a new way of organizing a company. Through training and use of intelligent workstations, work follows a natural flow from creative to routine. The cost justification for the augmentation hardware and software required to support this strategy is found in the financial contribution of future creative activities and applications. With principals free to perform more creative work, and with their creative activities augmented by technology, a business gains the ultimate factor for enhanced competitiveness in the world market: heightened white-collar productivity, especially by principals who are responsible for delivery of effectiveness and innovation.

As shown in Figure 4-12, in order for principals to tackle new business opportunities and challenges, they must be able to delegate their work to support personnel as it dynamically

Figure 4-11. Integrated work flow.

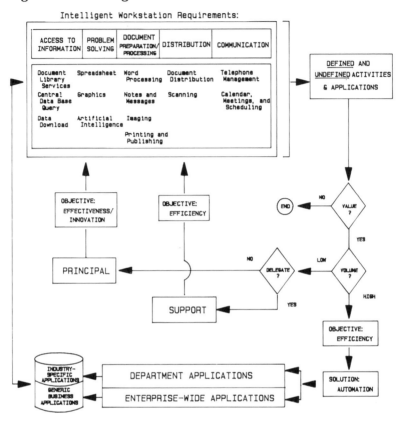

Figure 4-12. The WRM process.

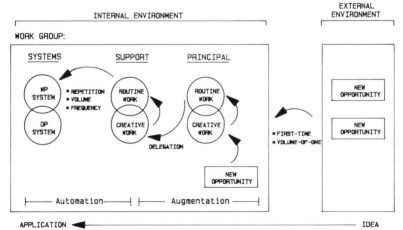

changes from creative to routine. Remember, the nature of work dynamically changes over time. When support personnel first absorb newly delegated work, it may be creative for a short while but quickly becomes routine. When this delegated routine work increases in volume, it can justifiably be automated. If it doesn't increase in volume, it remains with the support personnel. This is what we mean in the WRM process when we say "get the right work to the right person."

This new integrated system impacts on how we organize a business. Chapters 5 and 6 discuss these implications—how they will change the existing power structure as well as what the new role will be for the creativity-augmented manager and work force.

Chapter 5

Information as Power

In the past, a company's data processing department owned the automated applications. It owned the data and the channels for delivering the information, and it controlled the type of equipment, software, networks, accessibility to data, vendor resources, and so on. Today the seat of power has shifted to outside the data processing palace; power is now in the hands of PC users who have broken the bonds of automation and understand the augmentation implications of today's technology.

This chapter takes a look at power, what it is and how it is used in most businesses. We focus on the power that comes through access to information, and we see how it has changed with the introduction of the personal computer. We discuss the problems today's Information Systems (I/S) managers face, and we recommend a restructuring that provides a new role for I/S. This is the only assurance that automation and augmentation can be linked effectively throughout the corporation, thereby guaranteeing the productivity growth American business needs for the 1990s.

I/S—A Department in Trouble

Distrust, anger, bewilderment, hopelessness, fear, and animosity are just a few of the feelings that can disrupt an organization as it tries to implement technological solutions to white-collar productivity challenges. In the midst of this, the Information Systems (I/S) personnel have to deal with growing pressures: increased demand for advanced information technology, a growing shortage of skilled personnel, and resulting tensions between I/S and the users of its services. The base of power and the control of information systems are changing within the corporation, and I/S is losing ground.

Today, I/S managers face two- to four-year backlogs that are growing by 20 to 25 percent annually. The pressure is on to deliver information technology to end users more rapidly than ever before. More and more managers see the importance of using information technology to differentiate products or services as well. As one I/S executive recently described, "Historically, we have always been behind the curve in this company on how to use information technology competitively. Suddenly our senior management has realized that our company may not survive the nineties if we do not start using it better. So the race is on. We are so far behind, it is like riding an old mare, and now they want to go to the Kentucky Derby next week!"

Perhaps senior management gave I/S some mixed signals in the 1980s. Now that the race is on, I/S faces the added task of finding young people with the necessary skills to meet an increasing demand for information technology. The *ideal* programmer is a good listener, works well without constant supervision but also enjoys working with people, is sensitive but possesses a great deal of self-discipline and persistence, enjoys analyzing business processes and investigating new technologies, has some project management skills, is logical and an excellent communicator. Obviously, the job requires a unique set of skills.

Here is the challenge. The U.S. Bureau of Labor Statistics estimates that the number of computer programmers needed will grow from 570,000 in 1988 to 915,000 by the end of the century! That is a 60 percent increase! I/S managers are facing increased competition to find the very best candidates, groom them to be skilled application programmers, and entice them to stay with the company over an extended period of time. That is no small task. It may easily take one or two years before a new candidate really understands the business and is truly productive as a programmer. He or she then becomes a valuable resource in the market and must be given incentives to stay with the company. With a dwindling applicant pool, where are I/S managers going to get the talent?

Many will come from data processing's user community—people who already know different aspects of the business. That is good news, because actually it is far easier to teach someone how to be a programmer than it is to teach a programmer the inner workings of a business. Of course, advanced programming languages and computer-aided software engineering (CASE) tools will also help increase programming productivity, but the latent demand for more I/S services is so great that even these tools may make only a minimal difference.

Augmentation tools let workers fulfill many of their computer requests themselves. In other words, when professionals have an integrated system, they can fulfill some needs without employing a programmer. Facilities such as database query, download, and spreadsheet can sometimes satisfy up to 40 percent of users' demands.

Users of I/S services want flexible solutions because all of their work is not routine. It all cannot be precisely explained to a programmer. Managers are not asking for independence from the I/S organization. They simply are trying to tell I/S that traditional application solutions solve only some of their problems! They want some flexible tools that will enable them to use existing information better, whenever they need it, for whatever reason they need it. In other words, data processing customers are asking for help to *augment* the way they work, not just *automate* predictable routine work. Why? Because automation alone is only half the answer.

Providing end users with computing tools that augment work activities can be a frustrating effort for I/S managers. Many are not eager to assume the responsibility; they already face significant automation challenges. They are fully aware that many end users have gone off in their own direction and will not return. Others throw down the gauntlet to independent users, thinking, "Just wait until they need our help! Just wait until they want access to *our* data!"

A growing number of I/S customers have asserted their independence from I/S. In fact, the theme of a major technology firm's advertising campaign is that the traditional slow response and excessive resource requirements of I/S cannot meet the reactive or creative needs of business. As a result, the rising stars in business are buying powerful workstations and software without I/S knowledge.

Advertising may portray data processing personnel as experts who always make things too complex and are incapable of understanding user needs! What the end user generally does not know is that I/S is equally frustrated with the growing complexity of implementing workable solutions which must eventually be networked. The subtle message I/S hears is that end users are just as competent as I/S in determining solutions, and often do better without I/S involvement.

Dispersed technology, new networking capabilities, and advanced augmentation tools have resulted in growing I/S pressures and increased user demands. These factors are also changing the organizational power base. In the past, users of I/S services were a captive audience. They were the *recipients* of change imposed by automated systems often designed in a vacuum by data processing experts. Personal computers and augmentation tools have dramatically shifted the sphere of influence. They have empowered users to be *agents* of change. We will talk more about this shift in focus later in the chapter, but since it revolves around the matter of power, we need to pause and take a close look at this politically sensitive subject.

The Perception of Power

What is your emotional response to the word "power"? Is it positive? Is it negative? In should be neither. Power is simply the ability to influence someone's behavior to accomplish a specific objective. The objective may be positive or negative, but power is neither.

There are seven basic sources of power, or influence. We use these continuously, quite naturally, and many times subconsciously. We use them in personal relationships with our children, our parents, our spouses, and our friends and co-workers. Most of the time we use these sources of power without a specific plan or rationale, but we know that it *feels* right.

The seven sources of power are *coercion, connection, reward, legitimate, referent, expertise,* and *information.* Remember, however, that you have the ability to influence another's behavior only if you are *perceived* to possess the power and will use it. Power is dependent on the other person's perception of our power, not on our own perception of power.

1. *Coercion* is based on fear and intimidation. People acquire coercive power only if they also have an arsenal to follow through with their threats. The arsenal must be recognized as threatening and the person must also have a reputation for following through with threats. If people are going to use coercive power, they must clearly communicate their expectations and the consequences of not fulfilling the requests. They can easily lose this power if their demands

are inconsistent or if they fail to carry through with the consequences.

2. *Connective* power depends on association. In other words, it is not what you know, but whom you know. People acquire this power by nurturing personal and business affiliations that can be important allies later. Those who master this power are constantly considering the impact of their decisions on long-term business relationships. They usually are more willing to negotiate and compromise. They view requests for favors as opportunities to build valuable contacts. They demonstrate extreme political sensitivity and are nearly always recognized as team players. They use these carefully nurtured affiliations discreetly—only when relevant to the situation and when timing is appropriate. This power depends upon not only whom you know, but the perceived value of your connections and your ability to gain access to those connections.

Connective power can be quickly lost by losing favor with the contacts, by no longer having access to their resources, by not visibly displaying the connections, by failing to nurture those contacts, or by trying to use connective resources when not relevant.

3. *Reward* power or influence can be based on intangibles as well as tangibles. For example, if you are a purchasing agent, you may have the power to approve, prioritize, and initiate an acquisition for a typewriter, a personal computer, a more comfortable chair, an extra filing cabinet, or certain supplies. A manager may have the power to reward you with an office with a pleasant view. Of course, a manager also has the authority to sign a pay increase, a tangible asset that we usually relate to more easily.

The first rule in leveraging reward power is to appropriately match the reward to the recipient's needs. The second is to ensure that a short-term reward is consistent with long-term objectives. The third is to reward people publicly whenever possible. Every time you publicly recognize someone, you subtly reaffirm your power, not only with the recipient, but also with all who witness the event.

How do you lose this source of influence? You lose it quickly (1) if the reward does not match the person's needs; (2) if you reward a performance publicly but witnesses to the event believe the individual is undeserving; (3) if you reward everyone, even the marginal performers; or (4) if you reward someone when the recognition is overdue and anti-climatic. When you exercise your influence in any of these ways, people quickly perceive that your ability to use this power is unpredictable, frequently unwise, and, therefore, meaningless.

4. *Legitimate* power is also referred to as positional power. We all have some influence based on the responsibility and authority associated with our position in the organization. We can grow that power base by aggressively expanding our responsibilities, but there remain boundaries to our positional influence over others. If we overstep these boundaries, people quickly perceive that the demands are not legitimate. So, in order to wisely use this power, we must stay within the perceived boundaries, defined by the organization.

When using this power, give consistent guidance and direction. If a person is receiving certain directions or demands from one person and you place conflicting demands on the same person, the recipient becomes frustrated and may ignore both. Or you may lose this power if you fail to make decisions rightfully expected of you. If you have a tendency to make bad or contradictory decisions, you will lose the respect of others.

5. *Referent* power is based on mutual respect, on the sharing of common goals, values, activities, or interests. It is being sociable and genuinely caring for people. It encourages the open expression of feelings and is built on a willingness to be vulnerable. It is respect for the humaneness of others.

The result is that people like to be around you. You make them feel good! Your opinion is valued; they want to be liked by you and are willing to comply with your subtle requests for personal favors (not demands). They place value on your friendship, on your judgment, and welcome opportunities to enhance a relationship built on mutual respect. They willingly put in the extra effort at work when you ask because they know it is appreciated, not demanded, not coerced.

People with this power exercise it with genuine sensitivity. They seize opportunities to emotionally support others, and they do not hesitate to reinforce their friendship publicly. They ask for favors only if consistent with the common goals, common values, common bonds that have already been established. So, how does a person lose referent power? It is quite simple: by (1) acting like a jerk; (2) failing to publicly reinforce personal relationships when needed; (3) publicly discrediting or disavowing friendships; or (4) abusing the trust others have given.

6. *Expertise* is a power gained through knowledge or competency. If others do not perceive you to be knowledgeable and competent, you do not have this power. In other words, you may be the most brilliant statistician, the most skilled financial analyst, the most learned lawyer, but if you do not convince others of your competency, then your expert power is neutralized. Built on knowledge, competency, and experience, expertise must be translated into action, not just words. People must willingly share their expertise with others through patient coaching, guidance, and humility.

Occasionally, experts may want to dictate exactly what should be done. When disagreements and questions are treated with disdain and impatience, people are alienated and the expert's advice is no longer sought. The coaching and expert guidance must also be relevant to the recipient and to the overall business objective. If the knowledge or competency that a person is trying to share is not really relevant, his or her power is diminished.

This power can be lost if (1) you have expertise but do not willingly share it with others; (2) you unfairly challenge or discredit the valid credentials of others; or (3) your expertise is no longer relevant to the overall objective—that is, "the business has passed you by."

7. *Information* power is what this chapter is all about. People acquire this influence in two ways: (1) by possessing the actual data, or (2) by controlling the channels of information. People with information power know where or how to get the information that is needed.

To use information power wisely, you must (1) first assess the value and accuracy of the information; (2) sell others on the importance of the information; and (3) express a willingness to share desirable information when needed. If you control the data or the channels of information but others do not know it, your information is powerless.

You can lose this power (1) if you no longer have access to valuable information; (2) if you use inaccurate information and it negatively affects the performance of others; (3) if the information is no longer valuable or pertinent to others; or (4) if you deny access to the information without a valid reason. The result will be that others will not ask you again; they will find other sources for the information.

Power is neither good nor evil; it is simply the ability to influence someone else's behavior to accomplish a specific, desired objective. Now let us next examine how the Information Systems department's base of power has changed during the past few decades and try to understand why.

The Computer Gibberish Breakthrough

Twenty years ago, the data processing department in most companies typically reported to the controller or vice president of finance (and many still do), and the applications that were automated were mostly financial accounting systems and other very basic line-of-business applications (payroll, general ledger, payables, etc.). When the data processing department designed and programmed these processes, it often did it in a vacuum, with little participation from users. Why? Because the programmers were the experts. They were the only ones who knew how to make the computers work. The users' perceptions were that it must be complex because it *sounds* so complex: bits, hex, dumps, control languages, ABENDS (abnormal end-of-job), and so on—computer gibberish!

The less people understand something, the more they fear it. When they fear it, they can easily be intimidated. Many data processing customers were intimidated by the new technology. They were told how these new applications would change their jobs. Was that bad? Not necessarily, because that was how management and data processing understood their roles. They were the agents for change: Apply fixed technology to solidify and streamline business processes and make them more efficient.

After these new systems were designed, coded, and tested, they were delivered to data processing customers who were told what to do, what new data were now required, what reports they would receive, how frequently they could use their programs, how their new terminals would be used, how their job activities would change. This was coercion. The experts knew best; experts knew what could and could not be done with computers. It must be right! Besides, what choice did the end user have? The data processing professionals controlled *both the data and the channels of information!*

Were the majority of data processing professionals liked or trusted? Would you trust someone who was radically changing your job, your department's operation, without your participation? Data processing did not possess a tremendous amount of referent power; there was not a lot of mutual trust and respect.

How about reward as a power base? Suppose someone put a new computer terminal on your desk one Monday morning. He showed you a new way to key in the data, a new set of reports you were told to learn and use. He told you not to use your old method, even though you know it well because you have been doing it for the past twelve years. Now it has to be changed. Why? Because it will make you more efficient! Is the data processing terminal perceived of as a reward? It is a condition for continued employment. Data processing departments had three primary sources of influence in the 1960s and 1970s: (1) expertise, (2) coercion, and (3) control of both actual data and the channels of information. At this point, some readers may be saying, "But that's us now!" If this is the case, then you probably are far behind in delivering augmentation tools to white-collar workers and will be facing these changes quickly!

A Technological Revolution

What happened in the 1980s? The personal computer! Apple Computer Corporation started it and was later followed by IBM, Compaq, and many, many others. Why was this invention so important? Was it simply cheaper technology? These were not just desktop computers to automate payroll, inventory, or order entry. People discovered that these minicomputers helped them work more effectively.

As the speed of the personal computer explosion accelerated in the 1980s, these same data processing customers came home from work, sat down to eat a quiet family dinner, and asked their 10- and 12-year-old children, "What's new in school?"

"Oh, we're learning to program computers, Mom!" one says. "Yeah, Dad," the other chimes in, "you should see the really neat things that Joey and I learned to do on the screen. We made these graphs and. . . ." These same users went back to work and asked themselves some questions: "Why am I intimidated by this new technology? Just how complex can it be? I wonder if what the programmer told me yesterday about it being impossible to write a program for what I need was really true? I wonder how much a personal computer would cost our department, and if I can get it approved without I/S knowing about it?"

Managers began to question, listen, read, talk to their

friends, buy their own personal computer, experiment—to feel good with computers. "Hey," they told themselves, "that wasn't too hard. In fact, that was kind of neat! Even fun! Now if I could master these functions, I wonder if. . . ." Who is the expert now? Today, nearly everywhere we turn, we are bombarded with information technology—in shopping centers, in newspapers, on television. Through osmosis, we are all gradually becoming aware that we, too, can be computer experts.

Some users have been very aggressive, defining their own needs and acquiring their own solutions. Many end users even acquire their own departmental computers, set up their own local area networks (LANs) of personal computers, and write their own software. The I/S former power base of expertise has declined rapidly, and may continue to diminish into the 1990s. Likewise, fear, intimidation, and coercion are negated with a growing base of knowledge. What about the power of information? With their own computers, local area networks, personal computers, and access to public dial-up networks, end users have created their own data and control new channels of information. When reports from data processing do not agree with their changing requirements, they re-key relevant information into their own computers, enter new or additional data, and use augmentation tools or write short programs to meet their needs. The formal I/S department no longer tightly controls the data or the channels of information. It has lost much of this power because it has been slow to respond to end users' demands.

What about the end users of I/S services? New experts on technology and software began to emerge outside the I/S ivory tower. They were not data processing professionals and did not want to be. Some knew more about setting up local area networks, personal computer features and functions, and new augmentation software packages on the market than did many I/S professionals. They have enjoyed success where previous I/S attempts had failed, and have quickly shared it with upper management. As a consequence, their reputation has spread to departmental executives, their connective power links have lengthened, and they now control more data and alternate channels of information. They have also started to assume more legitimate ownership of their own application requirements, and they control more of their own destiny when it comes to improving efficiency and effectiveness. They have become agents of change instead of passive recipients. Table 5-1 shows the decline of power experienced by I/S departments in the past twenty years, as well as a projection into the next decade.

A New Power Base

End users will expand their connective power base in the 1990s if I/S management continues to satisfy only the routine needs of its customers with automation. This can be an opportunity for I/S to improve its power base. It must take a

Table 5-1. Shifting sources of power for I/S.

Source of Power	1960s & 1970s	1980s	1990s
Coercion	10	3	0
Connection	3	1	0
Reward	0	0	?
Legitimate	5	3	3
Referent	0	0	?
Expertise	10	5	0–3
Information			
Data	10	3	3–5
Channels	10	5	3–5

Scale: 10 = High Source of Influence
         5 = Medium Source of Influence
         0 = Low Source of Influence

proactive role in helping customers analyze their routine, reactive, and creative work needs, and develop an integrated augmentation platform for the corporation with better training. I/S must become business experts first and technology experts second.

This is no small task, and I/S cannot do it alone. Many departments are making progress in this area, but senior management must actively support an aggressive plan to ensure that its first-line operational management team shares its business expertise with the I/S staff. Senior management must identify and encourage end-user experts to pursue careers in data processing, to significantly enhance I/S's effectiveness in building a power base and to help balance the future skills shortage I/S is facing.

As end users assume more responsibility for defining their own information-technology solutions, as they enjoy more successes using augmentation tools and share these results with upper management, their legitimate power will continue to increase. I/S's legitimate power will depend on its ability to receive senior-management support for corporate standards for databases, networks, architectures, augmentation platforms (consisting of the fourteen basic and data facilities previously outlined), training, and so on; and to leverage both automation and augmentation for competitive advantage.

Now that end users are acquiring more personal computers and departmental systems, they are also becoming frustrated with the redundant effort of rekeying or recapturing information they know already exists in corporate files or databases. They want access now! This is an opportunity for I/S management to retain and enhance this information power, but the window of opportunity is getting smaller. If I/S does not provide easier access to data, end users will rapidly build their own duplicate and independent departmental and work group databases. Next, end users will informally network them together (many are already doing so). If I/S is not sensitive to this growing demand and fails to respond quickly, end users will not cooperate later when asked to use the official I/S databases and networks. Senior management and some I/S managers will again wonder, "What happened?"

If, however, I/S responds to end-user need for access to information, if it recognizes the dynamic nature and different types of work and the need for augmentation, if it aggressively develops better training, if it provides more responsive "help desks," these responses can be perceived as rewards by end users. Likewise, if common sense, sensitivity, and a willingness to be vulnerable, to negotiate, to proactively cooperate, and to understand business problems completely through the eyes of end users and chief executives become I/S attitudes, referent power may be established. It is partly Theory Y management. Office workers must be empowered with information and augmentation tools to do their jobs better. Doing so will have major impact on organizational change.

Automation enhanced the need for a well-staffed bureaucratic hierarchy to manage the system, feeding a midriff bulge in the corporate pyramid. Traditional automation inhibited rapid change because it solidified the defined organizational processes, centralized the legitimate power structure, and reinforced the formal and acceptable channels of communication.

Augmentation, however, breaks down those bureaucratic barriers that restrict the flow of information. One of the reasons we have called the augmentation tools facilities is that they *facilitate change*. They decentralize information and put it into the hands of operational-level workers, allowing them to be agents of change. Augmentation facilities support creative and reactive work. They enable first-line business operations (those closest to the customer) to be more responsive, to be more flexible and innovative, to better differentiate a company's services in the marketplace. As a result, the organization itself can become more fluid and dynamic in its challenge to be competitive.

Management in the Vanguard

To achieve the phenomenal increase in white-collar productivity that is available, American business urgently needs to define new roles for senior management, the I/S organization, and end users. It is the only way companies can fully benefit from the augmentation technology currently available and the tremendous information power clearly on the horizon. We discuss senior management's role as it relates to vision, strategy, organizational issues, and other elements in Chapter 6. At this point, let us look at what senior management should do in relation to I/S.

I/S and Business Strategy

Traditional I/S mentality has generally focused on technology, not strategic business planning. For senior management to expect I/S to develop an I/S strategy without understanding the business strategy is ludicrous. Senior management must communicate a clear vision of where the business is going and what challenges lie ahead, so appropriate productivity tools can be selected. Business strategy must drive the I/S strategy, but this can only happen if I/S is part of the strategic planning process.

I/S directors must be given the opportunity to expand their horizons, to understand the visionary perspectives of the CEO. They need to better appreciate the competitive challenges of the next ten years—as strategic thinkers and partners, not as technology hoarders. I/S management must understand that tomorrow's business problems will not be solved with traditional ivory-tower approaches. They must aggressively market and deliver productivity tools to end users and provide them with better training.

Technology for Top Management, Too

Senior management should not be intimidated by technology. It must set an example, and it should insist on a complementary executive support system (ESS), also known as an executive information system (EIS). (See *Executive Support Systems* by Rokart and DeLong, listed in the Further Reading section of this book, to find out more about ESS.) An executive support system does not eliminate the need for augmentation tools; rather, an integrated set of augmentation tools is the foundation for an effective and innovative executive support system. Providing additional intuitive, front-end interfaces controlled by a "mouse" or "touch" screens for senior management use, these facilities can help generate customized queries and graphics to analyze critical business indicators and perform further multi-layered, "drill down" investigative analysis.

Wise Investment in Technology

Top management must realistically assess what its I/S organization can deliver within budget constraints, and make sure it wisely invests in the infrastructure (skills, architectures, networks, etc.). Then the right technology can be put in place when it is needed for gaining a sudden competitive advantage. Also, successfully installing augmentation tools and properly training the end users are cooperative efforts between I/S and end-user departments. As work changes from creative to routine, I/S should be involved in the process. I/S must have senior management's support in developing tools and networks that (1) complement the dynamic and rapid redistribution of work and staffing requirements within the organization; (2) accelerate innovation and creative efforts with augmentation tools; and (3) assist with the automation of routine work.

Compatibility and Consistency

Senior management must understand that if employees are left to select their own augmentation tools, the result may be equipment and software that cannot be integrated or networked to achieve maximum productivity. I/S directors must have the authority to set corporate standards in a multi-vendor environment. They must be able to establish standards or guidelines end users must follow when selecting technology and software.

This can be very difficult when end users are knowledgeable about the technology as well as the software. They often exert tremendous pressure on I/S to support them while they remain unwilling to compromise. As a consequence, there are two, three, or four different software packages for spreadsheet, word processing, graphics, electronic mail, and so on within the same company (many times in the same department or work group). How many businesses could operate effectively with four or five different telephone systems, each with its own features, functions, and networks? The telephone is an augmentation tool for more effective communication. What would be the result if employees had to be retrained on the phone system each time they changed jobs within the company? It should be no different for software.

Long-Term Benefits

Proper augmentation tools and training help fulfill the vision for greater productivity, but investments in technology are not enough. If senior managers have a short-term outlook, or a quantitative approach to investments in augmentation, they may be disappointed. If managers expect immediate returns, they could be frustrated. Generally, the benefits of augmentation cannot be realized in three or six months—sometimes, not even in twelve months. It may take two or three years to fully realize the results. Remember that the goal is not simply to reduce or control cost, but to increase revenue, to improve service, to create a competitive edge, and to transform work itself! These things are not accomplished overnight.

A Dynamic Restructuring

Figure 5-1 shows a new view of the I/S organization supporting augmentation. At the top is the president, and just below is the CIO (Chief Information Officer).

The CIO must understand the business strategy and translate its requirements into a feasible I/S support plan,

Figure 5-1. A new organizational structure for effective I/S augmentation.

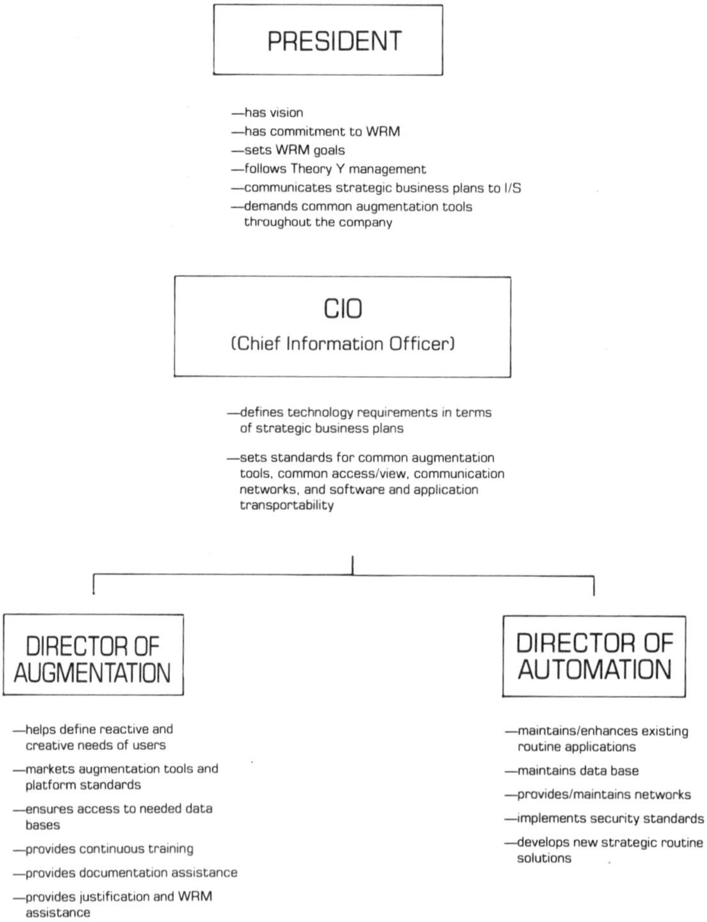

PRESIDENT

—has vision
—has commitment to WRM
—sets WRM goals
—follows Theory Y management
—communicates strategic business plans to I/S
—demands common augmentation tools
   throughout the company

CIO
(Chief Information Officer)

—defines technology requirements in terms
   of strategic business plans

—sets standards for common augmentation
   tools, common access/view, communication
   networks, and software and application
   transportability

DIRECTOR OF AUGMENTATION	DIRECTOR OF AUTOMATION
—helps define reactive and creative needs of users	—maintains/enhances existing routine applications
—markets augmentation tools and platform standards	—maintains data base
—ensures access to needed data bases	—provides/maintains networks
—provides continuous training	—implements security standards
—provides documentation assistance	—develops new strategic routine solutions
—provides justification and WRM assistance	

leveraging information technology for best competitive advantage. The CIO sets the corporate standards for automation. He or she also sets standards for augmentation with the user community, which is represented by the Director of Augmentation. At a minimum, standards should include a common platform of fourteen augmentation tools, common access regardless of hardware or software, the transportability of augmentation tools across a broad range of hardware configurations, and guidelines for supporting corporate networks.

The Director of Automation retains the traditional responsibilities of a data processing director, with a heavy emphasis on supporting the routine applications of the business. The director also creates, maintains, and makes accessible the resulting data in the form of easy-to-use relational databases. In addition, the director implements and supports the necessary networks and security requirements to meet both automation and augmentation needs of all users.

The Director of Augmentation aggressively helps all I/S users to define their reactive and creative work needs, assists them in selecting the appropriate tools, and networks these skills to leverage the effectiveness of others. It is the augmentation director's responsibility to interface with the Director of Automation to ensure that users have access to relational databases in a timely and complete manner. (If that cannot be done, then those user requirements are escalated to the CIO and the appropriate end-user executive until adequately resolved.) On a continuous basis, the director not only provides justification assistance for augmentation but also ensures that the tools used for innovation or effectiveness are documented, and that benefits are broadcasted to all who might gain from these ideas.

In this new structure, end users understand that they are solving individual and work group business problems with their choice of augmentation technology and software, but these choices must be fully integrated into a corporate network if the business is to achieve full competitive advantage. Remember, these tools facilitate the redistribution of work not only within work groups and departments but also within the company, because work is dynamic, not static.

End users must understand that they cannot encircle their work groups with walls of independence. They also have responsibility to understand the long-term business needs and to ensure that their data can be networked for maximum productivity. They must realize that as people move from job to job within the company, there must be continuity of software standards to avoid repetitive training and worker frustration. They must see that it is not individual productivity or individual technical expertise that counts but effective team work and cooperation.

Perhaps even more significant, the shift in information power discussed in this chapter will revolutionize the role of middle management in today's flattened organizational structure, because the control of, ownership of, and accessibility to information will be permanently changed. Former layers of excessive management can and will be eliminated in the Work Redistribution Management process presented in the next chapter.

Chapter 6
The Management Revolution

It is no secret that U.S. business has lost much of its competitive edge in world markets. We are fighting to regain our posture, but we have a long way to go before we are number one again. Here, at last, is a workable formula for success—a new management approach that trims the fat while it maximizes innovative potential.

The suggestions in this chapter may be radical for some; indeed, they call for a decentralized organization and a management approach based on individual development, trust, and fulfillment. To reach this point, we first look at how American business took on its characteristic top-heavy structure and how that burden has inhibited corporate growth. The alternative we offer replaces bureaucracy with customization, regimented work with creative endeavor, short-sighted management with individual and team work responsibility and initiative. At the heart of this formula is the integrated office software system described in Chapter 4 and administered through the reoriented I/S management discussed in Chapter 5.

The Work Redistribution Management (WRM) plan links all work to the strategic business objectives, then distributes routine and creative work to the appropriate persons. As an added feature, WRM is an effective means of measuring white-collar productivity in qualitative terms—information that can help a company identify poor performers and eliminate excessive management layers. Work Redistribution Management may well be the best way U.S. business can use today's information technology to meet the 1990s challenge of world competition.

Competitive Strength Comes From Increased Creativity

There is little doubt among business leaders that the bulging hierarchy of most companies must change. In fact, a change of nearly revolutionary proportion is being thrust upon us through new technology and the need to remain competitive. How should organizations change? We are not naive enough to think we can address all the nuances of reorganization in one chapter. We can make a few observations about how this inevitable restructuring will affect the shape and flexibility of American business and the major role that augmentation tools and networked knowledge workers will play.

During this century, technologies such as the telephone, television, plastics, the automobile, satellite communications, and so on have radically changed our life-styles, occupations, economic structure, and marketplace. Now business is on the verge of exploiting an augmentation technology that will revolutionize the way we work in the 1990s. For instance, although the use of computers in business is only about thirty years old, the development has been remarkable. "Data processing" dealt mainly with numbers and text until the early 1980s, when introduction of new technology (see Figure 6-1) accelerated. Today, the automation of routine work and the augmentation of creative work have the potential of greatly accelerating the development of competitive experience curves by giving the power of information to professionals responsible for creative work. In other words, when creative efforts are supported by augmentation tools, it increases the frequency of creating new experience curves with a substantial competitive advantage.

Competitive experience curves are not really straight lines. As Figure 6-2 shows, they look more like a series of downward steps, whereby creative work is followed by routine work in a progression toward lower unit costs and greater output. Note that innovation occurs only once in the experience curve when it is initially created, and then it is made more effective through additional creative effort.

The greatest competitive advantages come from either innovation or effectiveness, neither of which can be achieved without creative work. This is not to say that efficiency is not worthwhile. It usually is an objective only when activities or applications are already well understood, well documented,

Figure 6-1. Evolution of information systems.

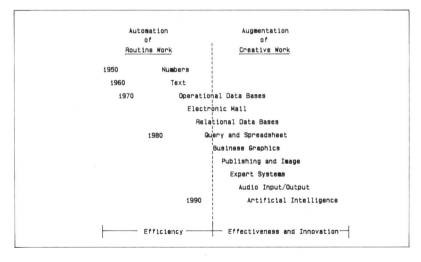

Figure 6-2. Competitive experience curve.

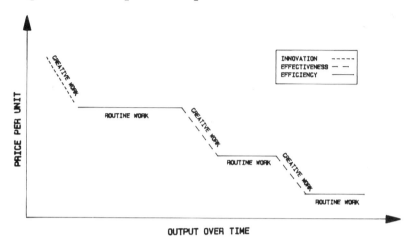

and appropriately delegated to clerical support personnel. Efficiency is also the easiest to be quickly imitated by a competitor and, therefore, is the least sustainable.

Faster hands were the ticket for cost strategies in yesterday's industrialized economy, but they will not sustain the competitive edge in today's international markets. Creative ideas that lead to product innovation or more effective service are what make the difference between surviving and anticipating or driving the market. To remain on top, companies have to set the pace, gain a sizable market share, or restructure the industry by changing the rules of competition.

Management is bombarded with emotional pleas to "use information technology for competitive advantage," as though it were a magic wand that could be drawn across the office to produce instant profits. There is much more to it than that. Technology can help a company stimulate innovation through creative effort, but even achieving that requires a corporate vision. Only then can information technology be leveraged for competitive advantage (see Figure 6-3).

Figure 6-3. Leveraging information technology for competitive advantage.

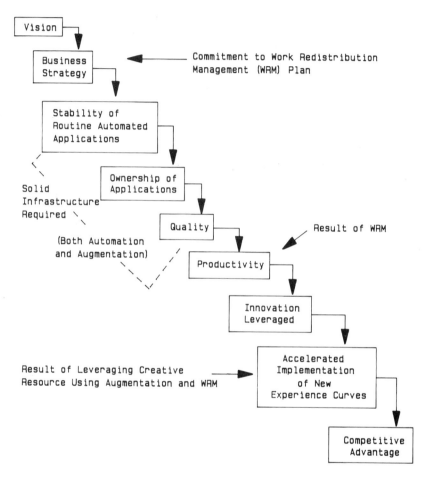

Vision at the Top

Achieving a competitive advantage starts with a *vision*. It is developed and nurtured by senior executives and communicated to everyone in the business. Visions, by their very nature, often are disruptive to current business processes, so they require conviction, persistence, and drive if they are ever to materialize. Visions are not easy to develop, nor are they easy to communicate, because they are new, unexplored ideas. Visions are not safe; they offer no guarantees of success, yet they may be the key to long-term survival. Visions often seem obvious, but if they were so apparent, they would already exist! They require strong leadership, with insight into future competitive forces, changing customer demands, work-force requirements, optimum management styles, and prerequisite corporate cultures. They call for the best organizational design to get the right work to the right people with the right tools, so the company can provide the best customer service in the marketplace.

Examples of vision statements implicit in this book include:

- All 40 million workers in U.S. offices need a personal computer.
- There must be one augmentation standard for systems and software compatibility.
- There must be a new approach to downsizing and managing work.
- The I/S organization must proactively support the need for augmentation in addition to traditional data processing.

In his book *Management Tasks, Responsibilities, Practices*, Peter Drucker lists four activities as necessary for making work productive:[1]

1. Analysis of specific operations, requirements, sequences, etc.
2. Synthesis of individual operations to form a cohesive process
3. Control of the process—direction, quantity, quality, etc.
4. Appropriate tools

Drucker emphasizes that, in order to make work productive, management must start with an end product, because a vision of the end product determines what activities need to be performed and what skills or tools need to be used.

A vision translates into a *business strategy*, which is senior management's plan to achieve specific objectives. The strategy encompasses the key elements for success and the critical factors for implementation. It starts with a focus on the customer and builds and maintains a solid infrastructure to support the business objectives—touching on skills, staff, management, corporate culture, organizational structure, and I/S support at a minimum.

From an I/S perspective, this infrastructure means that essential line-of-business automated applications are current and fairly stabilized and that a platform of common augmentation tools has been established for the enterprise and is in wide use. A solid infrastructure also means an organizational support system that gets the right work to the right people. It means new responsibilities to implement the vision. Long-term productivity occurs only after individuals take ownership of their activities and applications—when they are rewarded for having done so. Productivity also depends on consistent quality. It is only when these have been established that senior management can look for and expect innovation from creative efforts. Only then can synergistic, creative teamwork implement new, competitive experience curves for the company. That is a vision actualized.

Bureaucracy Strangles Progress

How many times have managers turned a deaf ear to employees and thought, "We don't pay you to think! Just do it." Or, worse, how many times have you said it yourself? There is a myth that in highly industrialized economies, bureaucracies are ideal structures because the primary objective is efficiency. In these well-defined environments, workers

are encouraged to become expert at one repetitive or predictable activity. This management style is not always appropriate. How many times have you reached your emotional
boiling point when an employee has said, "That's not my
job!" That response epitomizes the specialization and segmentation mentalities of the bureaucratic mind-set.

Why have we perpetuated the mythical quality of bureaucracy? Is it because companies have no clear vision of
their end product? Or is it because the right way—the most
efficient way—works? "Don't fix something that isn't broken." Does something have to be broken to make it more
effective?

Sometimes circumstances—the marketplace, people's
expectations, or whatever—change, and so an organization
must change also. For instance, our economy has shifted
from an agricultural-industrial base to a substructure of
services. We have seen rapid deregulation of certain indus-
tries and also industry convergence (for example, a bank
that is also a brokerage firm). In the past two decades, the
marketplace has expanded from a primarily national one to
an integrated international field. Turbulent financial ex-
changes immediately impact on diverse national economies.
Something else has happened, too. Products have become
more specialized to meet specialized needs, and quality and
better service have become the critical advantage in the
marketplace. Throughout the changes, management has
used the competitive forces of the market to influence its
organizational design; Figure 6-4 traces that evolution. Ac-
cordingly, it is time for that design to change again.

Evolution Is an Ongoing Process

We think of biological organisms as fixed in our time,
having evolved from their prehistoric forms over the centu-
ries. They continue to evolve and will be different yet again
in future eons. Likewise, we tend to view a business's organization of employees as fixed, as the way it has to be. If we

Figure 6-4. Forces impacting organizational design.

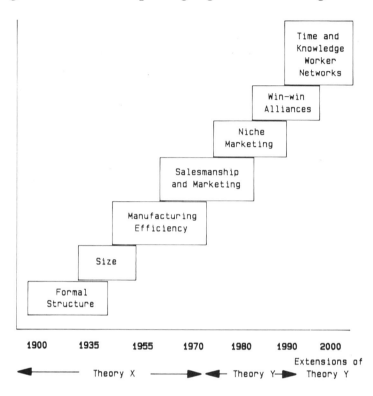

look at the past, we see that companies have organized themselves differently at different times.

In the early 1900s, companies grew rapidly with the emergence of domestic markets and began to formalize their structures. As expansion continued internationally into the 1920s and 1930s, size became critical to meeting increased demand. Higher-volume efficiencies could be best achieved by huge multi-unit organizations. What better example of this than the military hierarchies that brought us through the First World War? Hierarchical structures centralized to tighten management control and coordination were what the new business leaders had just experienced in the military. Along came Taylor, Cooke, and Weber to provide management with the efficiency-measurement tools and management theories to formalize these practices for the 1930s and 1940s.

During this era, workers were "economic-driven" entities who could be best utilized by reducing their activities to mindless, specialized tasks. "Faster hands" were expendable in this interchangeable production mode, and every activity could be measured for efficiency. The result, of course, was an antagonistic relationship between workers and management that provided just the right climate for unions to emerge.

In the early 1950s, a few companies quickly captured a market share with innovative products, primarily because their marketing was savvy. IBM was a leading example of a company that evaluated market needs and formalized its strategic planning process. The additional market research and the formalized planning and measurement systems in these companies fattened the staff and management ranks, and the professional "staffy" was born.

These top-heavy organizations began to limit their responsiveness to consumers and curtailed innovation. The bureaucratic planning and control process resulted in midriff bulge, which restricted these companies from responding to rapidly changing international demands. They also faced new competitors in the 1970s—small companies that went after niche markets. Con Edison, Ma Bell, IBM, GM, and others were attacked for their impersonalized customer service. These leaders were out of tune with the market; some even recognized it, but they could not change their organizations or "staffy" bureaucracies quickly enough.

In the 1980s, companies realized that being the low-cost producer was not enough. Products and services had to have (of all things!) quality. They had to offer more. Quality products had to be packaged with added services so as to erect high switching costs and differentiation barriers to fight off a flood of new competitors. This has resulted in the current wave of interorganizational electronic linkages and alliances for a new competitive advantage.

To achieve these objectives, companies tried to break

themselves down into smaller entrepreneurial units. They utilized matrix organizational structures and management. Mostly, they did not staff these structures with entrepreneurs—only more bureaucratic managers. When creative products or services did emerge from these quasi-independent entrepreneurial firms, the parent hierarchies often could not cope with the explosive success and quickly brought the smaller units back into the fold because they were getting too big and enjoying too much success!

The lesson learned in the 1980s, however, was that quantity measurements and mechanical planning are not everything! Quality, creative thinking, innovative win-win alliances, respect for individual workers and their ideas, participative management styles, and positive corporate culture yield exceptional competitive advantages. How can an organization leverage the creativity of its workers? How can it network knowledge workers to leverage innovation, to be more customer-responsive and service-oriented? Partly through Theory Y and participative management and also with a restructured organizational support system.

Theory Y at Work

Douglas McGregor's Theory Y gained momentum in the 1970s, but it took on more true believers in the 1980s, when many Theory X management teams faced a crisis. Management conversion to Theory Y is critical if a company is to break down its bureaucratic hierarchy into collaborative networks of knowledgeable workers.

Today's best management philosophy shows respect for the individual, believing that employees respond best to trust from management and that people respond well to a thank you or a compliment for a job well done. Applying Theory Y to creative work is obvious. But is it effective when managing routine work as well? Yes! The difference between Theory X and Theory Y is not the nature of the work, but the philosophy and practice used.

Management that fights this transition may not survive. Theory Y may need some extensions or modifications, but these will be defined as enlightened managers demonstrate visionary leadership and try participative styles, and as companies network their skilled workers to meet specific challenges. Work groups will be given the freedom to develop innovative solutions, and then be disbanded when the task is completed. It will be a new management style to meet a new competitive era that demands dynamic, flexible, and creative business practices. It is part and parcel of what we call Work Redistribution Management, or WRM.

Work Redistribution Management

The answer to increased white-collar productivity is twofold: better tools for leveraging brain power and teamwork, and better management to encourage creativity. We have discussed the technological link-up in Chapters 4 and 5, but it can only function in conjunction with Work Redistribution Management. (See Figure 4-12, "The WRM process.")

Work Redistribution Management is a new philosophy of managing work. It is a system for:

- Evaluating work in terms of strategic business objectives
- Classifying work as routine, reactive, or creative
- Distributing appropriate work to the right persons
- Automating routine work and augmenting creative work through an integrated augmentation software network
- Justifying the cost of investments in information technology and training for support personnel
- Measuring white-collar productivity, especially creative efforts

WRM recognizes work as a dynamic force, not a stagnant condition of office life. It provides a management enhancement process, with periodic evaluations of departments or work groups, to ensure that creative work is done by principals and routine work is done by support personnel. Through WRM, a business can utilize information technology to:

1. Improve white-collar productivity
2. Focus more resources on innovation
3. Trim the size of management and eliminate obsolete organizational bureaucracies
4. Improve the morale of workers through job enrichment and meaningful challenges
5. Accelerate change for competitive advantage by unlocking the creative powers of employees in a task-oriented, fluid organization

The Work Redistribution Management technique supports a Theory Y view of the business environment. It offers a tremendous return on a company's investment in people—especially in principals, its most costly asset. In WRM, competent managers understand how to build high-performance teams and how to cultivate and nurture creativity. They provide workers with integrated tools that foster high productivity, in a business environment that respects the individual and rewards good performance. The ultimate objective of WRM is to get the right job to the right person, and to do the work that has the highest strategic value to the company.

WRM requires a restructuring of the organization, which we have already shown is merely American business catching up with the evolving economic world in which we live. Some companies respond that they cannot or will not change their management practices. They recognize that this change may one day be required, but they refuse to accomplish the switch now. It is a lot like discussing the national debt with politicians. They all agree that something has to be done, but in essence say, "It's not my job." So, too, the productivity of white-collar workers in some offices will prob-

ably not be addressed until the company is on its last leg—
and then it will be too late.

The WRM Environment

In a bureaucratic organization, being an expert at routine procedures is not merely desirable, but an aspiration
actively fostered by management. This new era of customized, flexible services and products will demand that workers
broaden their tool kit with skills in many areas. The days of
"That's not my job" are gone. That is a philosophy that is no
longer beneficial to the employer, nor is it healthy for the
individual.

Think about the potential that exists when work, tools,
and training are properly delegated. Our case studies (see
Part II) outline numerous examples, but here is another. An
insurance division of a large financial group gave its secretaries a challenge, plus the tools to access formerly "sacred"
information. The secretaries began to access and modify
policy information such as addresses, renewals, premiums,
and the like, to better service customer requests and to
offload the sales agents of routine matters. As a direct result,
customers received more prompt service, the agents had
more time to visit clients and sell more insurance, and the
secretaries no longer felt brain dead from boredom.

In fact, secretaries in this insurance company now share
in a bonus if the agents increase their sales as a direct result
of the improved support structure. More important, support
personnel now view themselves as an integral part of the
sales effort because their view of their work has changed and
their work has become more exciting. In fact, the secretaries
are now also sales assistants, using such augmentation tools
as spreadsheet, graphics, query, and statistical models. Vision, a strategy, and WRM changed the way people work and
their expectations of excellent performance.

With slower growth expected in the U.S. work force and
escalating international competition, workers will have to
learn more skills to provide flexible services and customized

products. The business need to adapt and be more flexible will also demand that average employees be given more freedom to make meaningful daily decisions. The manager's role will change, and work groups will become the driving force for increasing productivity and self-management.

Management's new role will be (1) to open the channels for upward and lateral communications, (2) to provide an environment whereby responsibility is shared, and (3) to define a common purpose for work. Some essentials of this participative management are:

1. A common vision defined by senior management and clearly communicated to all
2. Goals and objectives set by each work group or department so the vision can become reality
3. Augmentation tools and a solid support structure to leverage each work group's innovative capabilities
4. Mutual respect and trust among managers, professionals, and clerical or administrative personnel
5. Freedom for members of each work group to select new members and establish its own measurements of success and excellence

These conditions will foster an environment where workers do more than just "put in their time," where they understand their contribution to overall company objectives and are excited to see the results. The Chinese philosopher Lao-tzu reflected this management approach in 600 B.C. when he wrote:

A leader is best
When people barely know that he exists,
Not so good when people obey and acclaim him,
Worst when they despise him.
"Fail to honor people,
They fail to honor you":
But of a good leader, who talks little,
When his work is done, his aim fulfilled,
They will all say, "We did this ourselves."

WRM Nurtures Creativity

Innovation will not be restricted to the products or services a company manufactures or sells, but will be manifest in the way people work and how their productivity is measured. Leaders must sensitize their managers to the inevitable struggle for power between (1) those fighting for centralized controlling and standard bureaucratic approaches to routine work and (2) those welcoming more decision-making authority, fewer rules, more risks, and more freedom to be innovative. The former always want a road map, the latter want to try something untested. Instead of fearing the unknown, the new superstars will learn from the old and welcome changes that stimulate the work groups.

For a creative person to flourish, management must accommodate the characteristics of creative work. For example, creative work is accomplished by individuals or small work groups of six or seven people. For a creative idea to reach maturity, it has to bypass bureaucratic structures. Either creativity can fight with bureaucracy and lose, or management can adapt a different philosophy in which creative ideas are encouraged and explored.

WRM demands participation and leadership at all levels, not simply within management ranks. The power of reward is not held exclusively by managers; it also belongs to the work groups. Work group members will have the authority to hire and fire members of the group, so as to build the best synergy for their own productivity. Work groups can recognize and reward their peers for participation, for their willingness to learn new skills, and for their leadership, judgment, creative alternatives, and innovative ideas.

Control of the work processes will no longer be constrained by hierarchical reporting relationships. All organizational levels will have access to augmentation tools that enhance high-performance team building, that network knowledge workers, that free employees from rigid communications channels, and that open new paths to creative ideas.

Senior management will recognize that these spider-web networks of work groups need less formal management control. Instead, the electronic channels and common augmentation tools will allow work to be dynamically distributed to the best resource, will slice through layers of organizational politics and management bias, and will let executives feel the pulse of their operations directly.

The Manager of the Future

Today, power is based primarily on position: on the ability to reward, to control the channels of information, and sometimes to coerce. Tomorrow's managers are cheerleaders and coaches. Their power is based on their ability to create harmony and synergy. They do not simply tolerate crazy ideas; they *stimulate and encourage* them. They trust that the individuals they have hired take pride in consistently doing the best they can. They do not drive individuals to perform; they create the best environment for excellence. They allow workers to participate in as many areas of the business as possible, and they welcome refreshing ideas unfiltered by the hierarchy.

Participative management leverages ownership and innovation. A hard-line Theory X manager does not have a role in this new world, but a benevolent Theory X is still appropriate for managing routine work. A benevolent Theory X manager uses rewards and incentives to achieve the standards agreed upon by both management and workers. The manager of the future must learn to distinguish between routine and creative work and not try to manage them the same way! Through WRM, the new manager will recognize that all work is not the same.

The Failure of Downsizing

Business objectives have shifted in the past few decades, from reducing costs to controlling costs, to increasing revenues, to expanding market share, to "Let us just survive!" As a company moves through these phases, it must also transform organizationally. Work Redistribution Management helps take it from a slow-response bureaucracy to a lean, innovative risk-taker. If a company is going to downsize in the 1990s, it must be careful! It cannot afford to repeat the mistakes of earlier years and cut the arteries of a support system meant to relieve principals of routine work. Likewise, across-the-board reductions in principals will not eliminate unnecessary work. That only aggravates an already tense situation and slams a lid on creativity. Downsizing can be a valid move, but only when there is an understanding of the power of information. Let us take a closer look at some downsizing drivers, then see how WRM can sort through the dilemma.

A Tangle of Management Layers

Corporate power structures have often been characterized by layers of managers who have access to sacrosanct performance measurements, financial data, and so on. These measurements were designed by a few financial, technical, or other specialists; gathered by layers of data technicians; analyzed by numerous lines of structured code maintained by technical specialists; then deciphered for senior managers to present to senior executives. Layers and layers of control, layers and layers of filters. Sometimes layers and layers of nonsense!

The result was a hierarchical, often fossilized, snail-paced organization where managers spent their time "managing the system." The data collection, editing, formatting, analysis, and reporting often led to distortion, delays, and more questions. Questions often triggered a repetition of the cycle to validate the original distortion of outdated and over-managed data "from the system." The business drifted along, largely unmanaged until problems erupted. In such a crisis, management responded with radical immediate action, and the answer all too frequently was "Damn the system, full speed ahead!"

Then along came the minis and the personal computers. Slowly, data were no longer sacrosanct. Some of the "non-elite" produced reports that were often more sophisticated and easier to read. The power structure had developed a crack!

Independent end-user networks have started to appear. Letters, memos, messages, and reports no longer travel slowly up the hierarchy, to be sifted, sorted, and changed at every level, and then slowly travel back down. Now, networks and augmentation tools are blurring the distinctions between management layers. Individuals are networking with individuals, and work groups with work groups, across divisional boundaries. The old organizational hierarchy is getting in the way. The multiple layers constrict and often duplicate an organization's ability to gather and distribute information rapidly. When management spends much of its time on routine or reactive-routine management of "the system," quick competitive response becomes impractical.

So we see many companies eliminating professionals and managers to reshape or streamline their business. A few are doing it right, but most are simply reacting. They do not understand the problem; they know only that they have too many layers. They hope that by eliminating some excessive layers, they will restructure work as well.

Downsizing management and professional staff *does* have merit, but the essential problem is not the people. It is the failure to analyze the work, to get the right work to the right people, and to provide the right productivity tools. Most downsizing does not correct the imbalance of principals to support personnel we discussed in Chapter 1, nor does it supply the adequate augmentation tools we outlined in Chapter 4. In fact, it usually exacerbates the problem, so the productivity of people remaining in the organization decreases even more.

These approaches to downsizing have a tremendous negative impact on an organization's ability to be innovative and competitive, but the effect will not be visible until the mid-1990s. If some principals are eliminated, much of the creative work they were doing simply falls through the cracks and is not seen again until someone in the future finds the need for it, perhaps because the business has suffered from a lack of creative effort. Also, when a company offers downsizing incentives such as early retirement or other financial packages, who is eliminated—top performers or poor performers? Top performers are the most likely to volunteer for such incentives because they are the most skilled, the most confident, and the most likely to easily find another job. There is possibly another reason. They could be unhappy with inequities in the current workload, be irritated by the lack of administrative support for their work, or be weak from the struggle to acquire augmentation tools that could make them more productive. Many professionals to whom we have talked express frustration with senior management's apparent inability to comprehend their situation.

Such downsizing seldom eliminates work at all. If it does, it is usually creative work, not routine. Instead, most downsizing unintentionally results in more routine work being done by the remaining professionals and creates hiding places for poor performers who now are "too busy" with routine work to take on the challenge of creative work.

WRM to Measure Productivity

If you wish to downsize, build a new paradigm that gets the right job to the right person, and provides the best equipment for each job. Next, determine if the *low* performers are also *poor* performers. (They are not always the same, as the second case study shows.)

If you decide that certain employees are low performers but not poor performers, then it is a choice between traditional downsizing or increasing the productivity of those low performers. At least you will have used WRM to set the stage by having built a work environment to encourage productivity, and having provided the tools to accomplish that goal. With WRM, top performers emerge into the spotlight. Peer pressure, not management pressure, usually causes the downsizing to occur as a natural recourse—in an environment that, at the same time, leverages creative work.

If, after establishing the new paradigm, you find that the lowest performers are also poor performers, then your choice is to:

- Downsize—Lose poor performers through attrition and *do not replace.*
- Increase productivity—Lose the poor performers through attrition and replace with potential good performers. You will be able to judge their contribution because the WRM plan will be in place.

Remember, a business must restructure work, not just eliminate people. It must provide the appropriate augmentation tools and the right management. Companies must literally knock down these sacred power structures and reshape them into knowledge-based networks where decisions are made at increasingly lower levels and where there are enough support personnel to free principals for creative work. This can only be done with an integrated augmentation software network and Work Redistribution Management. Only then will companies discover and implement new competitive experience curves at an accelerated pace and be more competitive in the years to come.

Chapter 7

The WRM Process— How to Make It Work for You

The time has come to transform WRM theory into practice. After all, any idea can sound exciting, but what good is a theory if you cannot put it to work for you? This is a practical chapter. We move from general guidelines to specific procedures for making WRM a reality. The case studies in Part II also reinforce these procedures through concrete examples, and we recommend that you select and read at least one of these case studies before going further. In the end, you should be able to use WRM to fine-tune your business and move toward greater white-collar productivity.

Seven Steps to a New Management of Work

The WRM analysis is basically a seven-step process:

1. Explanation of program to department managers and work group members

2. Completion of work diaries by all employees
3. Initial review of diaries
4. Interviews with employees to complete data collection
5. Data entry and reported results
6. Interpretation of data, prioritization of work, and redistribution if necessary
7. Presentation of final report

On average, since the dynamic transition of work from creative to routine follows a nine- to twelve-month cycle, the data collection and interpretation steps should be repeated at regular intervals. Before we get into the mechanics of the analysis, let us consider the initial presentation to sell the idea to senior management.

The Presentation to Top Management

The materials in Chapters 1 through 6 should be sufficient to assemble a presentation of WRM principles to top management, as well as to department managers and other key figures in the company. Remember that WRM is not a short-term effort; good management and meaningful change always require vision and commitment. However, the technique is not difficult and does not take excessive time. The effort can be easily justified in terms of overall increased productivity results.

Table 7-1 is a review of the time it takes to institute WRM in a typical department of 40 people, including the initial management presentation. The return on investment (ROI) justifies the time spent on this analysis. For example, the ROI for a company using this technique for the first time has averaged a 30 percent increase in productivity among principals. With a department of 40 people, in which 35 are principals and 5 are support personnel, the results are shown in the following calculations:

Table 7-1. Schedule for implementing WRM and WRM resources.

ACTIVITY DESCRIPTION	WHO	EVENT TIME	NUMBER OF WORK DAYS
■ TOP MANAGEMENT PRESENTATION	M	2-3 HOURS	1
■ DIRECTOR/MANAGEMENT PRESENTATION	M	2-3 HOURS	1
■ WORK GROUP TRAINING PRESENTATION	C	4-6 HOURS	1
■ DATA COLLECTION - FILL OUT WRM DIARY	P	2-3 HOURS	5
■ INTERVIEW PREPARATION	A	20 HOURS	3
■ CONDUCTING INTERVIEWS	C	30 HOURS	4
■ DATA REDUCTION:			
● DATA ENTRY - 1 HOUR/PARTICIPANT	A	40 HOURS	5
● COMPUTE RESULTS	A	2 HOURS	
■ DATA ANALYSIS	C	2-3 DAYS	3
■ DRAFT FINAL REPORT	C	2-3 DAYS	3
■ FINAL PRESENTATIONS:			
● WORK GROUP PERSONNEL	C	2-3 HOURS	1
● MANAGEMENT PRESENTATION	M	2-3 HOURS	

M = MANAGER   C = CONSULTANT   A = ANALYST   P = PARTICIPANT

■ WRM ANALYSIS FOR A WORK GROUP OF 40 PEOPLE TAKES:

	TOTAL TIME	NUMBER OF WRM ANALYSES PER MONTH	NUMBER OF PEOPLE
■ MANAGER	3-4 DAYS	2	80
■ CONSULTANTS	10-12 DAYS	1	40
■ ANALYST	6-8 DAYS	2	80

■ THEREFORE, A WRM TEAM COULD PERFORM:

WRM TEAM	ANNUAL COVERAGE
■ MANAGER - 1	
■ CONSULTANTS - 2 = 80 PEOPLE PER MONTH = 960 PEOPLE PER YEAR	
■ ANALYST - 1	

■ A WRM TEAM'S ANNUAL CAPABILITY:

■ 960 PEOPLE DIVIDED BY 40 PEOPLE PER WORKGROUP, EQUALS 24 WORKGROUPS PER YEAR, PER WRM TEAM

35 principals × $50,000 = $1,750,000/year

5 support × $20,000 = $100,000/year

30% principal productivity increase = $525,000

$525,000 ÷ $1,850,000 = 28% ROI

Certainly this ROI makes initial investigation of WRM worth considering. On average, a team of implementers can evaluate 18–24 work groups per year. That means evaluating the work of 720–960 employees per year.

The WRM Analysis

Assuming top management has given the go-ahead, it is time to institute Work Redistribution Management. The process begins with an introduction to those concerned. All members of a work group are included: management, non-management, and support personnel. In addition, if supplemental or "temporary" employees are used, their work should be evaluated as well. Bear in mind that the entire WRM process can be administered by qualified in-house professionals; outside consultants are not necessary.

Step 1—Explanation of the Program

In introducing the WRM program to the department managers and work group members who will be recording their daily activities, you need to emphasize the objectives of WRM. After all, it is only through such analysis that the right job can be given to the right person, and the proper organizational structure can support this new way of working. People want to excel if given the opportunity! They want their work efforts to be measured and recognized so long as they are measured on what they were hired to perform and are given challenging activities.

When we have introduced the WRM concept to groups in our research, the reactions have been the result of three influences:

1. *Reputation of the company.* Does the company treat its work force as a valuable asset or as a dispensable commodity? Does the company believe in the unique importance of people? The company must not have a reputation of justifying technology investments simply on the basis of a reduction

in headcount. Increasing productivity must be perceived as positive.

2. *Reputation of the manager.* Are managers perceived in a positive way? Are they genuinely concerned with their staff? The manager must come across as honest, understanding, and fair to all.

3. *Tone of the presentation.* Employees know when the mood is sincere and supportive of their efforts and when their input is honestly and confidentially respected. In addition, the first work group that uses WRM sets the response for other groups. If the analysis and the changes are perceived as positive, the following work groups will respond positively.

People understand the difference between routine and creative work, between work that is breaking new ground and work that is boring. The WRM analysis can help them enjoy their work more, and with this understanding they will cooperate in the process.

Be certain to make clear that all information gathered in the survey is confidential. Assure participants that if they disagree with a finding or a fact in the WRM process, the disputed matter will be deleted from the final presentation. No serious disagreements have ever been encountered once all participants are assured that individual responses are absolutely confidential.

Step 2—Completion of Work Diaries

The heart of the analysis is the Work Redistribution Management Activity Diary, a two-hour recall log. It highlights the activities and applications each individual does during the workday. With minimal instruction, workers can classify their activities as either routine, reactive-routine, reactive-creative, or creative. Management, of course, must agree with the classification; if an employee is unsure of a classification, management should offer help. Appendix C is a complete Work Redistribution Management Activity Diary. The first three pages give complete instructions for filling out the information. In addition, Appendix B offers additional guidelines. As you will see, the diary covers five days' work, each day broken into two-hour sessions. It is filled out once every two hours during the day, and all activities and applications performed during the two-hour periods are checked off in the book.

A two-hour recall method was selected after much experimentation. Experiments ranged from having a consultant follow an executive around all day, marking down each activity, to measuring thirty-minute, one-hour, two-hour, four-hour, and eight-hour work periods. When the results were compared, it was found that on an average, the two-hour recall method captured 90 percent of the same information as did recording of the executive's full-day activity by a consultant following the executive around all day.

Thus, the two-hour session was deemed equally accurate and more practical. This same method is being developed for personal computer entry and also in a vest-pocket version for follow-up studies.

Begin the analysis by having your initial work group use the recall diary for a "typical" week. This provides uniform accuracy across all work groups and starts you off with a detailed activity profile. If the week selected is not typical, you risk collecting inaccurate data and resulting misinterpretations. We discuss these problems later in the chapter, in regard to the interview.

Filling out the diary initially takes only three to five minutes every two hours. That is only fifteen to thirty minutes a day. Some people express concern for how much time the diary involves. After the first day, however, respondents quickly become familiar with the format and it usually takes less than three minutes every two hours.

The instructions in the beginning of the diary are detailed and should cover most questions. If people work more than an eight-hour day, they use the collection device for up to ten hours. If their workday is longer than ten hours, have them use the last period to cover all the time over eight hours. Respondents sometimes hesitate when they first see the diary, mostly because the forms cover a broader range of activities than they perform. We find that the average principal fills out only two items every two hours, and the support person about five items every two-hour period.

Employees should not take the diary with them when they travel, even if such travel reflects a typical work week. The point of the initial study is to identify work performed in the office.

Support personnel should have no problem classifying their work. However, principals sometimes find it difficult to designate their activities as routine, reactive, or creative. For guidelines on dealing with these special situations, see Appendix B, which goes into a little more depth on addressing these issues.

Step 3—Initial Review of Diaries

The completed diaries are sent directly to the individual conducting the study. This individual, or analyst, can be any skilled professional within the company; he or she need not be part of top-level management. The analyst looks at each entry and notes any questions, missing information, and inconsistent or unclear responses. Then the analyst schedules interviews with each of the respondents.

Data from the diaries are beneficial because they profile how people spend their time—in other words, the percentage of time spent on routine or creative work. But the diary in and of itself does not indicate *which* activities and applications can be delegated or *what* work requires new software or greater computer connectivity. The element of WRM analysis that puts these aspects into focus is the interview.

Step 4—Interviews With Employees

The interview process averages thirty to forty-five minutes per person. However, interviews for support people generally are shorter, while meetings with some executives can take as long as two hours. To allow for these time differences, it is best to set up interviews every forty-five minutes, and stagger support personnel with principals. In our example of a forty-person work group, we averaged one hour each, or a total of forty hours to complete the interview process.

There are four important objectives to the interview process. First, interviews are used to resolve questions about data in the diaries, to ensure that accurate information is entered into the computer program. Second, further information can be gathered to define and classify the applications done by the work group *if this has been requested by management.* In other words, you may be asked to capture samples of applications and label them as routine, reactive-routine, reactive-creative, or creative. Third, you need to understand and concur with the labels employees have given their work—what they have marked as routine, reactive-routine, reactive-creative, and creative. Fourth, and most important, you need to build a list of "To Do's," which are the creative activities workers feel they should be doing if they had sufficient time. (There is more about To Do's later in the chapter.)

It may be appropriate to ask individuals to bring a copy of each application performed. This is particularly true of new departments or new companies. For example, if the department is still evolving, management may literally not know what is being accomplished in detail. Having a copy of every application can help explain why employees devote their time to certain activities.

During the first part of the interview, one should review questionable data and correct them specifically. For instance, the form entitled "Typical Week" should be checked. The Typical Week form should have been filled out during the initial work group training presentation. The first part of the form asks individuals to estimate how they currently spend work time; the completed form should represent a "typical" week. It can be filled out in terms of hours or percentages—whatever is easiest for the person.

The second part of the form asks the individual whether he or she would like to spend more time or less time on each activity. These responses are then compared to each person's daily entries for unusual variances. Normally, if a principal wants to spend less time on an activity, that activity should be labeled as routine in the daily part of the diary. If a principal wants to spend more time on an activity, the chances are the work will be labeled as creative in the daily portion.

The rest of the interview involves a series of questions to put the data collected in perspective. We provide some of these questions later in the chapter, but let us return now to the next step in the analysis.

Step 5—Data Entry and Results

Once the interviews have been completed, any corrections to the work diaries are made so the information can be accurately entered into the PC WRM program for analysis. We estimate that it will take one person forty hours to enter the data and one person two hours to run the program.

Step 6—Interpretation of Data

The computer program gives the results of the study in graphic form, and now the reports must be interpreted by the person who conducted the interviews, since only that person can put the data and the interview results in perspective. The interpretation will lead to the final presentation and recommendations in the distribution of work. You will be required to consider what the capability is of the support personnel in your office. Are they properly trained? Do they feel as if they are part of the team? Do they like to be challenged? Are they eager to learn? Can they absorb this delegated work or must you hire additional people?

If the study shows that four man-days of principals' activity can be delegated, the following rule of thumb will provide improvement opportunities: About 70 percent of principals' routine work can be delegated. Some of this work may be absorbed by word processing centers or by modifying existing data processing applications. In addition, the augmentation tools will increase productivity. The result may be that four man-days of routine principals' work can be accomplished by two support personnel.

However, if one or two people are providing support for ten or twelve professionals, it may quickly become impractical for them to absorb all the delegated work. Instead, it will become necessary to increase the number of support personnel and add proper integrated office software support tools to increase the efficiency and effectiveness of the support structure.

It is also imperative that management understand the activities performed by support personnel in the same work group. Any routine work *with volume*, currently performed by support personnel, should be delegated to data and word processing centers. This off-loads support personnel so they can assume new activities that should be delegated by principals.

If there are additional tasks to be performed that can be delegated, extra support personnel should be hired. Remember: Get the right work to the right people; why have a $50,000-a-year principal perform work a $20,000-a-year support person can accomplish? Remember also that the job descriptions of support personnel will change the quickest. If the ratio of principals to support people is out of balance, correct it by initially hiring more support personnel, not more principals, and delegate the routine work that principals are performing to the additional support personnel.

In summary, the WRM process analyzes office work and prioritizes current and known future requirements. The new priorities are based on strategic business needs that deliver measurable, meaningful results. However, you cannot accomplish all this work in the first six to eight months. People need time to adjust, change, and accept new challenges. New work cultures need time. This initial process concludes with the presentation of the report, but this is in essence only an interim report. The WRM analysis should be repeated in six to eight months to measure the gains in white-collar productivity that have been achieved after implementing the recommendations.

Step 7—Presentation of Final Report

Once the work group members agree with the final presentation, it is reviewed with management. Once it is accepted, implementation of the recommendations can begin immediately. The initial thrust should always be *first* to get the right work to the right people and rebalance the support system. The *second* is to get the right tools (equipment and software) for the right job.

General Interview Questions

The following section is a general guide of questions that will help provide the more detailed information you may want to understand after analyzing the data. The interviews will help you understand what activities and applications fit the routine and creative definitions. These insights allow you to explain to management specifically which work should be delegated and which should remain with the principals.

1. *How long have you been in your current position?* Remember, new personnel will categorize a great deal more of their activities and applications as creative since they are in the middle of their learning process. Be aware of this and make

sure your interpretation of the data is sensitive to such factors.

2. *Is your work in any way cyclical?* If so, how and why? What portion of the cycle were you in during the study week? These answers can influence the results. For example, a study was done in an audit department that had a three-week cycle. During the first week, the auditor spent time collecting information. The second week was for analysis, and the third week was presentation preparation and delivery of the results to management. Be sensitive to such cycles *before* starting a study. If you find a cyclical pattern to the work, as described in the audit example reviewed later in this book, spread your WRM collection over the complete cycle by starting different people on different days throughout the entire cycle.

3. *Was the week of the study a typical one?* If not, what was atypical? Ask about specific tasks, activities, and applications. Determine the work type, and see if anything unexpected happened.

There is nothing worse than being "blind-sided" by the fact that the week in question was atypical and, therefore, invalid. It can happen, but if you are aware of such factors, add a few more days for gathering data in the diaries to achieve a typical profile. That does not mean, however, that you have to be overly sensitive about some of the people categorizing their week as atypical. If you find a large majority of the participants fall into a typical category, review this fact with management and take the appropriate actions.

4. *Is the department staffing satisfactory?* Ask whether it is over-staffed, under-staffed, or adequately staffed. Do people have any special skills? If so, what skills?

Answers to these questions may come when interviewing managers, but it is also an excellent question for work group and department principals. There often are strong feelings about uneven workload distribution in the group of which management is frequently unaware.

5. *How do you perceive your time overall?* To help people give correct feedback to this question, let them make small,

simple decisions, as opposed to complex, interrelated ones. For example, ask them to tell you how they spent their time, divided between routine and creative work. For example, "What percentage of your day is spent on routine work?"

6. *How do you handle disruptive work?* Disruptive work interrupts a person's plans for that day and supersedes them. For example, suppose the date for a presentation to the vice president is moved up two weeks, leaving less time to prepare. That is disruptive work, and it can greatly affect productivity (either positively or negatively). What percent of your work is disruptive? How much of the disruptive work is creative? How much is routine? Remember, by definition this work is also reactive, so the work is either reactive-routine or reactive-creative.

7. *How much work do you delegate?* The percentage of time spent on routine work relates directly to how much work can be delegated, but it is not necessarily an accurate reflection of *all* work that could be delegated.

8. *How much creative work can you accomplish?* Determine how much of a person's creative work is reactive and disruptive. In addition, always ask how much creative work can be delegated to support personnel. The answer should be none, if the person understands the concept of creative work. If you get a response other than none, it is always good to ask what the work is and why the delegation is possible, because it may be routine work with a low volume.

9. *Tell me about your job description and job responsibilities.* This request allows respondents to think about what they actually do and, in their own words, describe their job. To help people describe their responsibilities to you, it is often helpful to review their current written job description. Also ask if they have a list of annual objectives, short-term/long-term objectives, appraisal objectives, "hot" projects, or current To Do's that may not be in their formal job description.

10. *What could be done to improve the operations of your work group?* This question often provides good insights into activ-

ities and applications that build a To Do list. Another, more direct question would be: What should your work group be doing that is not being done today? Most people answer this question quickly with a list of activities, applications, or ideas.

11. *Are you satisfied with your administrative and secretarial support?* More than half the people asked may answer yes, they are satisfied with their current level of secretarial support. The next question, then, is, "What support do you receive from your secretary?" The answer is usually "mail support." Mail support means secretaries open the mail and put it in a file for the principals, who then pick it up at their leisure. So your next question should be, "Do you have any other support needs?" The answer to this may be no. The problem is that support has eroded slowly but surely over the past thirty years, so that people cannot recognize the needs they have and assume many of the routine activities that can be more efficiently and less expensively performed by support personnel.

12. *Do you have any general problems or concerns?* Find out if there are any problems like training, access to information, use of personal computers, or workload imbalance issues.

13. *Do you feel you are doing the right things?* Explore whether employees feel they are performing the right activities and applications. Could their time, energy, and skills be used more effectively? If so, doing what? Why?

Management Questions

There is also a set of questions to ask management during the interview process, so as to compare actual work priorities and contributions to key business strategies, and to ascertain the Theory X or Theory Y profile of the manager.

Keep in mind, however, that the intent of WRM analysis is to determine if the right person is performing the right job in the right way. The ultimate objective here is to identify the routine activities and applications that principals perform and that should be delegated to support personnel.

To stimulate a manager's thought process to identify new work that could be done if time and personnel permitted, ask questions such as the following:

1. Suppose your manager gives you two additional principals. What would you have them do?
2. Are you feeling any pressures in your work group? What kind of pressures? Any of the following?

- Excessive backlog
- Attrition
- Decrease in accuracy
- Rapid growth
- Lack of space
- Part-time/overtime imbalances
- Short deadlines
- Decline in quality
- Loss of profit
- Limited budget

3. Are the people in your group all experienced or relatively new? How many are experienced? How many new? Who are they?
4. Are there any situations (i.e., personnel) of which we should be aware or to which we should be sensitive during our interviews?
5. What are the major activities, applications, and functions for which the work group is responsible?

The "To Do" List

Making up a To Do list is part of the analyst's job during the interview step. Ultimately, it becomes important for the final report. Here is a word of caution. What one firm considers a To Do, another may regard as a basic management or employee activity. In other words, it may be easy to question any item on a company's list. What is important to realize is that each company's business strategy is different, and each company is in a different stage of its growth cycle. A company creates its own activities and applications through normal growth and evolution. If there are not any To Do's, this is a work group in which downsizing may be an appropriate answer. In our research and WRM analysis, we have yet to find a work group that could not identify a critical list of To Do's. This is important information to gather before implementing any downsizing efforts.

The following is a composite list of actual To Do's from previous WRM studies. The management teams of these companies considered these items to be high-priority (creative) opportunities for their firm at this time.

- Implement a cash-flow management program with controls, schedules, and periodic reviews.
- Construct a financial-management procedures manual.
- Develop a standardized pricing system and strategy.
- Analyze the department profitability and productivity.
- Develop guidelines for department overhead versus revenue generated.
- Develop and implement a department-driven budget system.
- Develop a quality assurance program.
- Develop a demographic analysis program that will determine market segmentation, needs, revenue, potential customers, etc.
- Perform more complete personnel analysis—pay structure, retirement programs, benefits, cost analysis, program funding to prepare for various acquisitions to follow.
- Develop the capability to automatically look up addresses, phone numbers, customer balances, agents, representatives, employees, etc.
- Develop the capability to access computer data, such as customer information, employee information, financial information, etc.

- Prepare a curriculum for training and employee development.
- Develop a policy manual for the integration of acquisitions.
- Create an easier way to prepare presentation materials such as overheads and graphics.
- Prepare a department budget tracking and allocation.
- Improve the quality, coverage, and timing of audits.
- Develop new training programs for security, auditing, teller operations, branch management, clerical roles, etc., to ensure standardization of all acquisitions.
- Eliminate duplication of efforts in maintaining personnel records.

Management perceives these items as activities that must be accomplished for the business to stay healthy and competitive. These To Do's require the creative efforts of management and staff professionals. WRM opens the way to identify and achieve these goals.

Periodic Reviews

A repeat of the WRM analysis will enable the company to determine the following:

- The effect of WRM efforts on revenues and profits
- Which To Do items should be continued and which discontinued
- The effect of the new management process on time saved, resulting in quality of work, and on overall work behavior

This second WRM analysis is best conducted about 6 to 9 months after the work groups begin using the new support system, after there has been time for individual growth to take place, and after many previously creative activities and applications have been classified as routine. By this time, those "new" routine activities and applications will have been delegated to support personnel.

On the second set of interviews, the original questions generally are still applicable, but some should be modified to recognize the benefits of WRM. For example, all personnel should now have an intelligent workstation with appropriate augmentation software facilities and should be able to identify work changes that affect their productivity. You will need to determine what software is being used and whether it is consistent within the work group. Since there may currently be more than one vendor's software for a given function, the following will guide you through the interview. Have the person complete this form concerning the software on his or her personal computer.

Personal Computer-Based Software

	Use (L/M/H*)	What Software?	What Applications?	R/C
Word Processing	__ / __ / __	_____	_____	__ / __
Spreadsheet	__ / __ / __	_____	_____	__ / __
Graphics	__ / __ / __	_____	_____	__ / __
Telephone Manager	__ / __ / __	_____	_____	__ / __
Query	__ / __ / __	_____	_____	__ / __
Other	__ / __ / __	_____	_____	__ / __

*L = Low, M = Medium, H = Heavy

Have the person do the same for any host-computer software.

Host-Based Software

	Use (L/M/H)	What Software?	What Applications?	R/C
Database Query Facility	__ /__ /__	_____	_____	__ /__
Database Download Facility	__ /__ /__	_____	_____	__ /__
Electronic Mail (messages)	__ /__ /__	_____	_____	__ /__
Document Distribution	__ /__ /__	_____	_____	__ /__
Calendar	__ /__ /__	_____	_____	__ /__
Scheduling Meetings	__ /__ /__	_____	_____	__ /__
Programming Languages	__ /__ /__	_____	_____	__ /__
Other	__ /__ /__	_____	_____	__ /__

Make certain you understand the individual's definition of low, medium, and high use. For example, use this chart:

	Hours	*% of Workday*	*% of Week*
High	_____	_____	_____
Medium	_____	_____	_____
Low	_____	_____	_____

Be aware there is an ongoing controversy as to whether software should be personal computer-based or host-based. Creative work demands quick turnaround time, and consequently needs a different type of support; this work is best augmented by an intelligent workstation. In light of today's technology, creative work is best done on personal computer-based software, while routine work with volume is best suited for host-based software. I/S departments normally are insensitive to creative needs not part of their traditional thinking. So equipment and software solutions obtained through I/S may not be most suitable. This I/S lack of differentiation between routine and creative work is widespread owing to a general lack of understanding of routine and creative work, so be sensitive to it.

Once you have inventoried the software being used and have prioritized the activities and applications, ask the following questions:

1. How many of these applications did you accomplish before you had the personal computer?
2. How much time did they take without the personal computer? What is the productivity difference before and after?
3. How many activities would you *not* be able to perform if you did not have the personal computer?
4. Are there some examples of how the new integrated office software has made a difference? Time saved? Revenue increased? Employee productivity differences? Work group time savings? Application or activity cycles shortened? Competitive advantages?
5. What additional software do you need? Can you get it? If not, why?

Before and After Comparisons

To grasp the changes that WRM and an integrated office software system have made, identify a few key applications and activities and determine their importance to the work group and their overall value to the business. Recognize the time and number of people it took to perform the work prior to the system versus the time and number of people after the changes. The productivity figures are usually rather amazing.

Next, identify the creative activities and applications. Distinguish between:

- Those that could not have been performed without a personal computer—a relational database, a query, a spreadsheet, presentation graphics, and so on
- Those that could have been conceived of and maybe even started but not completed as effectively
- Those that were creative, but became routine, and should now be delegated or already have been delegated to the support system (personnel and/or equipment)

In addition, quantify work group or company revenue, productivity, expense, and/or profit changes.

Compatibility and Transferability of Information

A critical problem to look for during the second WRM analysis is an inability to transfer information from one personal computer to another. Most businesses today feel it is the work group's responsibility to choose the software it wants. *This is unworkable.* I/S management should set the standards for augmentation software and hardware (see Chapter 4).

Therefore, the most common and palatable recommendation is for work group members to use any software they wish as long as the work stays within the group. If the work must be transmitted outside the group, it must be communicated using a corporate-wide standard. During the WRM analysis, examples of software and hardware non-compatibility must be documented, highlighted, and presented to senior management to prove that corporate standards must exist.

Obviously, it takes time to adapt to a totally new philosophy of management. "Keep it simple" is the key approach in the beginning. Most companies and most departments have the same initial problems. There are many activities and applications that are obviously being done by the wrong people. Correct the obvious first and, in the process, learn the WRM philosophy and process. Let employees gain confidence that management is working in their best interests as well as in the interests of the company. Of course, management must make the decisions to enact new activities and applications. WRM simply provides the management information to better make that determination.

Use the WRM process to document any increases in creativity or work effectiveness and to determine the value of the process itself. Ultimately the value of Work Redistribution Management will be recognized by all. For real-life examples of the value of WRM that provide in-depth coverage of concepts mentioned in this chapter, see the case studies in Part II. For more about measuring the productivity results of WRM, continue on to the next and final chapter of Part I.

Chapter 8

A Fair Day's Work for a Fair Day's Pay

As we have seen, many businesses throw technology at a problem long before they understand the situation. This book is concerned with productivity—specifically white-collar productivity. Certainly, productivity cannot be increased until it can be better measured. Rewards and incentives cannot be given until standards are set. Yet it is astonishing how little time most businesses give to these matters when they concern office work, especially the work of principals.

This final chapter considers the matter of standards and measurements for a fair day's work. We look at how much time is left in an average day, after all the breaks and interruptions are totaled, and then we give some ideas for maximizing that time. We take a look at some past theories of measuring output, and then use WRM and Theory Y to set new, more effective standards for today's office environment.

A Net Workday

What is a net workday? It is the amount of time a business person can reasonably expect an employee to actually work. Do you know how much time that is for your employees? You may say, "Eight hours each day, forty hours each week!" Not so. You may pay them for the amount of time, but this is not the amount of time they actually work! Is it the same for a support person as for a principal? These answers depend a great deal on your understanding of routine and creative work.

A normal eight to five workday, with one hour for lunch, leaves eight hours for work. To arrive at a net workday, you need to understand the normal office events that affect the calculation. For example, most organizations provide for four types of interruptions: breaks, fatigue, unavoidable delays, and personal delays. A fifteen-minute *coffee break* is normally allowed in the morning and in the afternoon. This is cut-and-dry, but the three remaining factors are variable.

The *fatigue* factor often is arguable. Originally, it was allowed in factories, where heavy lifting and other strenuous work were involved. During long hot summer days, fatigue was real in the sweltering heat and frequently still is in some jobs such as construction or in steel mills. In air-conditioned offices, where light, non-physical work is performed, it has been argued that the fatigue factor is not relevant. Slowly, businesses have grown to understand that constant typing, heavy telephone use, steady work on a calculator, or uninterrupted writing can cause mental fatigue. It is just as real as physical fatigue. Someone once said, "Thinking is hard work; that is why so very few people do it!" Most companies now allow a standard of 5 percent or 6 percent for fatigue.

The third factor is *unavoidable delays*. Suppose you have been called to a meeting with eight other people; two of them are late and the meeting is delayed twenty minutes. That is an unavoidable delay. Or a scheduled personal meeting with your manager is delayed while she finishes an urgent phone call. So you wait outside her office, talking to the manager's secretary for fifteen minutes about your disastrous trip to see your in-laws last weekend. Another unavoidable delay.

Unavoidable delays should not be confused with reactive work, which is disruptive in nature. Reactive work may result when someone interrupts you to ask for help:

> "How can I get reimbursed for this expense?"
> "Do you have a more recent telephone directory for headquarters?"
> "How do I charge a call to Europe?"
> "Could you immediately search the files and find last year's sales projections versus actual performance by product class?"
> "The copier is broken. Call someone now!"

Fulfilling these requests results in performing actual work. Unavoidable delays do not produce work—they only delay it. For example, your terminal is on-line to the mainframe computer. You are almost through with entering a complicated product order that has taken thirty minutes. There is a power surge, the lights flicker, the system goes down, and all your data are lost. Or, someone hurriedly rushes past your desk and accidentally bumps you with a cup of hot coffee. You drop the freshly typed fifty-page proposal that was in your hand and the spilled coffee lands on top of it. A standard allowance of 5 or 6 percent lost time for such unavoidable delays is not unusual.

The fourth factor is *personal delays*. We all need unscheduled rest room breaks. Occasionally, we need to take medication, or refresh our appearance, or simply get a drink of water. A standard allowance of 5 to 6 percent is frequently used.

There is one additional factor. Most personnel managers agree that there are unplanned emergencies. These may be interruptions owing to a family situation, such as if your child has a dental appointment or becomes sick at school and you need to leave work early to pick him up. There may even be a fire drill! In fact, the tenants of a recently completed business office averaged one false alarm per week during their first few months of occupancy. Each alarm took about thirty-five minutes from the workday.

In addition, workloads often cannot be precisely anticipated or distributed. For example, a telephone receptionist may have slack time on Wednesday and Friday afternoons in the summer, because most customers like to take off extra time for golf or other recreation. Or the clerical order-entry work may be light the first fifteen days of the month, but heavy during the last five days. Generally, a standards consultant allows 7 to 10 percent of total time for such emergencies. This leaves an average available net workday of five hours and thirty minutes:

Available Hours (in an 8-hour workday)	Allowances
— Two breaks	:30
— Fatigue break (5–6%)	:29
— Unavoidable delays (5–6%)	:29
— Personal delays (5–6%)	:29
Subtotal	1:57
Emergencies (7–10%)	
— uneven workload	:33
Total	2:30 non-work time

8:00 Available hours
2:30 Non-work time
5:30 Net available hours of work

Management and Standards

A business has to control and maintain the net workday. Typically, an organization hires people, gives them each a job description and a place to work, and provides normal supervision, meaning the boss does not ask every thirty minutes, or even every two hours, what has been accomplished or if there is some difficulty. For example, suppose you are a sales manager. You have a meeting every Monday, from 8 to 10 A.M., with your salespeople to review activities, objectives, and concerns. After the meeting, you may talk to one or two of them on the phone, but you may not see them again for a week. This is not unusual when managing professionals.

Or, suppose you are the manager of a word processing center. You hire a new person, train him on the equipment (if he is not already qualified), give him a number of drafts from your backlog, and then probably do not talk to him but once or twice a day. Likewise, if you are a data processing programmer, your manager gives you a user request from the engineering department and tells you to investigate it, perform the systems analysis, and design and report the results. Two weeks later, you review the flowcharts with your manager.

There is nothing inherently wrong with this approach to management; its success depends on who is being managed, the nature of the work, and how the person best responds to different degrees of attention. But as a general rule, people work at an average output rate of only 50 percent of their net workday, or 2 hours and 45 minutes of actual work. If you want more than 50 percent of a net workday—that is, more than 2 hours and 45 minutes of real work—there are two steps to take: First, set a work standard, and second, manage or supervise to that standard. When you set a standard and manage to that standard, you stand the chance of achieving 100 percent of a full net day (5 hours and 30 minutes) of work.

Work can only be measured against established standards, but can standards be established for all work in the office? Are work standards dynamic or static? In the mid-1920s, Lowery, Maynard, and Stegmarten, at Westinghouse Corporation, initially proposed that an average standard of performance could be established based on one's skill and desire or effort.[1] They recommended a "leveling" or "skill and effort rating" procedure of standards based on *definitions of skill and effort levels*, rather than arithmetic standards for motions required to perform a given task.

Later, in 1948, Maynard, Stegmarten, and Schwab, in their book *Methods-Time Measurement (MTM)*, described a "procedure which analyzes any manual operation or method into the basic motions required to perform it, and assigns to each motion a predetermined time value which is determined by the nature of the motion and the conditions under which it is made."[2] Based on predetermined time values, this method of studying motions used a new unit of measure called Time Measurement Units (TMUs), and it made it possible for the industrial engineer to economically develop new standards, especially for factory activities.

In 1961, MTM-based standards for clerical activities were described and given the name Master Clerical Data (MCD), in an excellent book on work standards called *Measurement and Control of Office Costs*, by Serge A. Birn, Richard M. Crossan, and Ralph W. Eastwood.[3] It also used TMUs, since their premise was that nothing can be produced without body motion: "Until a human being makes a motion, nothing happens."

While Birn et al. acknowledged that the productivity of certain office jobs could not be measured (comptroller, sales manager, purchasing agent), owing to their high degree of decision making, they went on to explain that even Einstein's creative ideas were of no real use until they were documented (motion) and communicated to others. Their contention was that the MTM approach of precisely measuring and analyzing each motion of office work (which may require multiple variations) was impractical and meaningless. Their reasoning was that when people perform office work, unlike factory work, they seldom use the same motions every time, not to mention that time and motion are *not* applicable to creative work efforts. Instead, they use similar *groups of motions* that can have time values assigned to them.

Birn and his colleagues pointed to a common mistaken theory of work that says if an activity costs so much at one volume level, it should cost proportionately more or less as the volume increases or decreases. They explained the flaws in such logic:

> The fallacy is the belief that what one did do is what one should have done; nine chances out of ten, this is not true at all. Hardly ever is what one did do, cost wise, what one should have done; and until one knows what he should have done, his costs are out of control and will remain that way. Again, we must recall that controls are only as good as the measurements upon which they are based, and past performance certainly is not a measurement in any true sense of the word.[4]

In 1961, this was a rather bold step. Birn, Crossan, and Eastwood modified the measurement process for factory work and adapted it for office work. Their logic was based on the assumption that work in both the factory and office was basically the same and that the majority of office work could be measured. These work standards applied to repetitive work with volume, as on the factory floor. In fact, Birn et al. recommended that the MCD process of measurement start "where the most people are involved in the most routine type of work."

This is common sense if you believe that the labor costs associated with routine work are the greatest expense in your business. However, as we have pointed out in Chapter 1, in most businesses today, the largest salary expenses are for principals, not administrative or clerical support. Principals should perform creative work, not routine work, if a company is to get the best return on its investment in people.

MCD treats all work as having the same value because what has value is not the end product, but the volume of right work activities—the "motions." Productivity with MCD is achieved when individuals perform the optimum set of various groups of motions—not necessarily faster, but more consistently throughout the day. In our WRM approach, the essence of productivity is in getting the right work to the right people and the right equipment tools for the right job and in leveraging the principal to perform more creative work.

Standards for Routine Work

Just as in a factory environment, you can apply standards, increase supervision, or use incentives to raise output of routine office work when it has sufficient volume. Let us use a simple example in which only one application is accomplished: A typist types purchase orders. The narrow job description keeps the number of activities at a minimum, making it easy to establish productivity standards.

Each purchase order takes an average of fifteen minutes to type. During a net workday of five hours and thirty minutes, twenty-two orders should be completed. Assuming a $10 an hour wage, you may quickly (and erroneously) assume that each purchase order costs $2.50 to complete:

5.5 hours × $10/hour = $55/day ÷ 22 orders = $2.50 each

However, the employee is paid $80 a day for a fair day's work of twenty-two purchase orders, so the purchase orders really cost $3.64 each. Unfortunately, you may not receive twenty-two purchase orders each day. When people work, they usually perform at an average or above average rate. With normal supervision, people generally work only half the time. Therefore, you can expect only eleven purchase orders a day—at a cost of $7.28 each.

Is that a fair day's work? Probably not. A fair day's work is the performance or output agreed upon by management and employee. Since we are discussing routine work with high volume, standards can be based strictly on historical averages if a company firmly believes that "what one did do is what one should have done." Or it can be established by using MTM or MCD methods. Standards, then, establish a basis for evaluating employee performance of routine work. They define a fair day's work that is higher than the average output normally supervised, not because the motions are faster, but because the frequency of activities is more predictable and consistent throughout the day.

There are three methods of influencing and controlling routine productivity without the use of technology:

1. More than normal supervision of activities
2. Measuring the activities against an established standard
3. Using an incentive plan

How can management supervise to ensure that the standard of twenty-two purchase orders is completed daily? It could provide supervision in the immediate area at all times—for example, in a word processing center, an airline reservations central office, or a directory assistance center. Or, when training individuals for the job, management can subtly mention that an average performer completes twenty-two purchase orders a day, and then reinforce this with a practice exercise showing how easy it is to complete one in fifteen minutes.

All of a sudden an *informal* standard exists. People can be praised as well as recognized for meeting the standard. To enact this informal reward system, management monitors and supervises performance on a consistent basis. With close supervision and an informal standard, a company could realize the full potential of twenty-two purchase orders a day.

An Incentive Program

The next step in controlling productivity in the office is an incentive program. Assume that management is willing to offer an employee 1 percent more pay for 1 percent more work. With this incentive program, it is generally agreed that realizing 120 percent of a fair day's work is a realistic but difficult goal to achieve. Remember, twenty-two purchase orders can be completed in five and a half hours, and now a company wants the administrative clerk to complete 20 percent more work, or 4.4 more purchase orders. The resulting incentive pay would be $16 (20 percent of $80, or 4.4 purchase orders × $3.64).

Of course, a rare individual may become very efficient and exceed even the normal incentive expectations. Consultants agree that 150 percent of a fair day's standard is considered to be a maximum upper productivity limit with any formal incentive system. The work that is produced in this type of system is highly repetitive, is very routine, follows a rigid format, and has high volume. This type of environment may be the step just prior to automating this activity or application.

Standards for Creative Work

As we have shown, standards can be set for routine work, but what does a company do about measuring creative work? Does the same management style apply? The value of *routine* office activities can be jointly estimated by management and the consultant, systems vendor, or industrial engineer. But only management can perceive the value of *creative* work. The actual value is not in the effort or motion itself, but in the end product or application that results.

Businesses generally expect principals to spend the majority of their time on unique, creative challenges or on infrequent, spontaneous demands that interrupt normal business. It is not possible to establish a standard that a principal must daily respond to twenty-two complaints about erroneous purchase orders. Nor can management tell an engineer that he or she must design every new building in two days. Predetermined time or motion standards cannot be applied to principals because the creative and reactive needs of a business cannot be consistently predicted. Managers cannot foresee everything that should be done, when it should be done, how it should be done, and who should do it, especially if they do not devote enough time to business planning. (Our experience is that managers generally cannot find enough time to plan and do things right the first time, but always have enough time to do it over.)

Can there be any measurements for creative work? Definitely. For example, salespeople can be given annual or quarterly quotas. Unlike routine work, sales do not increase simply by going through a pre-defined set of motions faster. They come from talking to the right people, listening attentively, asking the right questions, knowing the company's products, as well as those of the competitor, being well organized, knowing what to propose, and so on. The procedures for this are not concisely defined, but they are implied through management philosophy.

A principal's value is measured by the value of his or her results. A company cannot automate creative and reactive-creative work, but it can provide tools that augment the principal's ability to make the work easier, faster, or better. If companies give principals the proper set of augmentation tools, then they *imply* that these tools should be used when appropriate to increase productivity.

Here is an extreme example. A principal has a telephone on his desk. He could close the door and conduct personal business on the phone. He could make personal long-distance calls. He could take the receiver off the hook when he comes to work in the morning and put it back on just before leaving. The procedures imply that this office tool should not be abused. What is the value of a principal's phone conversation? That depends on with whom they are talking, on the topic, on the result minus the cost, on whether it was the best way to handle the matter, and so on. A business cannot justify the telephone until someone uses it. The same is true of all office tools that augment work.

The important goal in measuring creative output is to develop the synergy to leverage a work group's productivity, not just that of two or three individuals. The key is not "eliminating unnecessary work," as the business executive we quoted in this book's introduction proclaims; that is a short-term mentality. Instead, management needs an attitude that focuses on increasing revenue by enhancing creative work.

Birn, Crossan, and Eastwood implied that neither the factory nor the office produces a great amount of "new" work, so the two environments are analogous. That is wrong! The truth is that creative work *does* occur in the office. Normally in the factory, the creative work is known as research and development. But these research functions are physically separated from the routine manufacturing process, whereas in the office, creative work is integrated with routine production activities. This brings us back to the point established in Chapter 1: All office work is not the same.

Creative work comes from the list of To Do's, uncovered through the WRM process. The cost justification comes from tracking and measuring the benefits that result from accomplishing the To Do items. *Productivity* is a word that has been worn thin from overuse and under-definition. Nevertheless, it remains a crucial goal for all businesses. Productivity comes from ceasing to do work that is outdated and useless. It results from the time saved in using augmentation software tools. It comes from having direct access to computerized information, from delegating routine work to support people, by getting the right job to the right person. Productivity results from a management philosophy that places importance on people and customers, by managing routine and creative work in a positive way.

PART II
Seven Case Studies

The following case studies are actual business situations. They have been chosen to illustrate the flexibility of Work Redistribution Management. Remember, WRM is nothing more than a formalization of solid, day-to-day management practices. By the way, this process can be used by both private and public sector organizations with similarly successful results.

A Hospital's Executive Board
A Computer Company's Marketing Department
A Brokerage Firm's Audit Department
A Nuclear Engineering Company
A Computer Company's Advertising Department
A Manufacturing Company's Costing Department
A Petroleum Company

A Hospital's Executive Board

This case study shows how WRM works in the public sector, for a group of executive board members. This is a hospital that tried Work Redistribution Management to make its operations more effective and innovative.

Background

The hospital was successful and profitable. It had excellent data processing and word processing systems. Like most intelligent and resourceful executives, the board had cost justified its automation equipment with a reduction in support personnel. Thus, the president had two secretaries; six key executives (principals) were supported by one secretary; and the remainder of executives were in work groups with principal-to-support ratios from 10:1 to 17:1.

The board was extremely proud that it had been able to

control costs by tightly restricting any increase in support personnel. The philosophy was typical: The higher the ratio of principals to support personnel, the better. Needless to say, we had to be sensitive, because WRM emphasizes the delegation of low-value, routine work. Many times this requires management to rethink its principal-to-support ratios. However, this was an excellent group of executives and they responded very warmly to the challenge.

They decided they would like to try WRM analysis even though they were skeptical that it would show much. They understood the concept, but did not see how their work and responsibilities could be analyzed, "because they were different." They decided to experiment with the WRM analysis using their executives and support personnel.

First Analysis

The result of the first WRM analysis yielded the breakdown of time shown in Table II-1.

When the executives saw the data, they focused on how much of their time was spent with Communication, the majority of which was meetings. They said to the president, "We told you so. We have too many meetings and many of them are a waste of our time!" The president immediately

Table II-1. Distribution of executive time (percentage of total time).

	Routine Work	Creative Work	Total
Access to Information	1	1	2
Problem Solving	13	6	19
Document Preparation and Processing	3	2	5
Distribution	2	–	2
Communication	42	30	72
	61	39	100

responded, "You are absolutely correct. We will not have any more meetings without an agenda, and the majority of items had better be creative!" He started to understand the implications.

The executives previously had complained that they spent so much of their time in meetings, there was little time left to accomplish priority work. Until now they had no proof. Now they had a convincing argument. It appeared that each was reluctant to criticize peers for the poorly planned agendas and material presented at meetings. Now they had a consensus and could talk about the problem.

An immediate benefit was a decision that each meeting have an agenda with each item classified as routine or creative. The actual time spent in meetings could be reduced by sharing routine notices, announcements, and reports electronically, rather than consuming valuable meeting time. This resulted in a 25 percent savings of time, and they all acknowledged that this finding alone justified Work Redistribution Management.

The second issue raised by WRM analysis was that so much of the executive's day involved routine work. The president asked for examples of "routine" activities and two came to mind. The first was preparation for an upcoming centennial anniversary celebration.

One of the executives was spending 31 percent of his time researching and writing a history of the hospital. This document would be used for newspaper coverage of the event, for publishing a pamphlet on the hospital's history, and as source material to prepare the president's speeches during the week-long celebration. The president became upset that the executive's expensive time had been so negatively impacted by work which he (the president) considered routine. He had expected this to be assigned to a support person. As the discussion progressed, it was discovered that no one else was available.

We asked the following: "If you had mutually agreed that this project was either routine or creative, how would the situation have been different?" The president thought for a moment, then said, "From my perspective, there would have been no misunderstanding! He would have clearly understood that he had better get someone else to do it. If no one was available, then he would pay someone outside the hospital to do it on a contract basis. We've got far more important problems to work on." It was agreed that classification of the work would have helped ensure getting the right job to the right employee.

The second example of time-consuming routine work came up while reviewing the differences between routine and creative work. One of the board members was a heart surgeon. I asked the surgeon how he would classify open-heart surgery. I thought he would say that it was creative. Instead, he said it was routine. He explained that he had performed in excess of 2,300 open-heart surgeries, and that the first few cases were highly creative, but as he performed more and more, they quickly became routine. He went on to say that his first case involved over 15 hours in the operating room, extracting the vein from the patient's leg, opening the chest cavity, opening the pericardial sac, placing the patient onto the bypass support system, surgically performing the bypasses themselves, and then reversing the whole procedure. He remembered this operation as one of the most creative fifteen-hour events of his career.

After 2,300 operations, however, most of the process had become routinized. Today, specialized teams perform the individual steps; the surgeon comes into the operating room only to perform the actual bypasses. Then the surgeon made an interesting observation: "I am paid my fee in the event something out of the ordinary [reactive-creative] happens during the procedure. Then my skill and experience are required to assist this critical [reactive-creative] process." Even surgical work is dynamic, not static, in its nature!

Next, we analyzed the activity of the five support personnel in this work group. The executives found it interesting that 88 percent of their support personnel's workday was spent performing routine work. They thought that, at their level, administrative support personnel would have more challenging work. They did not realize that so much of it was structured, repetitive, and well defined. The executives started to realize that their ability to delegate challenging work was restricted by the high volume of routine work already performed by support personnel.

The executives were clearly uncomfortable with the idea of adding support people. They decided to wait and see. Another WRM analysis was performed fourteen months later to determine whether the process was working.

Second Analysis

In the first analysis, principals were spending only 39 percent of their time on creative work (see Table II-2). The second analysis showed that much of their routine work had been delegated, but since no additional support personnel had been hired, their activities were even more structured than before. This was not a healthy situation. When no more resources are available, routine work would again back up onto the principal's desk.

The second analysis also showed that 99 percent of support time was now spent on routine work. The current support system was saturated.

The hospital needed to hire more support personnel. The type of support person it needed was unique. The work group needed support people who could work with a personal computer and augmentation tools such as a relational

Table II-2. Comparison of results—two WRM analyses (in percentages).

| | First Analysis | | Second Analysis | |
	Routine	Creative	Routine	Creative
Principals (8)	61	39	44	56
Support (5)	88	12	99	1

database, a spreadsheet program, a presentation program, and a text program to prepare reports for the executives. Generally, these are not considered support activities, and the educational system does not train support people to perform these jobs. The nature of work is changing. Today, that person may be a young college student; college graduates can easily be trained as administrative assistants. As they mature and learn, they may evolve into principals. Business is changing fast because of personal computers and augmentation tools. Companies—public or private—have to change with it to increase white-collar productivity, lest we all fall by the wayside. The executives were convinced. They began adding support personnel and the proper augmentation tools to get the right job to the right person.

Augmentation Tools

The WRM analysis showed growth in the constructive use of the hospital's databases. Access to Information applications were slow to occur, mostly because of inaccessible data. With the implementation of the WRM workstation solution and the implementation of a relational database, the hospital's data began to be used more frequently by the principals before the second WRM analysis.

As an example, the business function of Problem Solving incorporates a variety of activities. It can involve a response to a difficult customer or personnel situation, or it can be putting together a formal presentation from data extracted from a relational database. Problem Solving can also be the creative design of charts used in a presentation. For the executives in this hospital, a fairly dramatic change took place.

Originally, Problem Solving occupied 20 percent of an executive's time, most of which was routine work. In the follow-up analysis, 28 percent of the time was spent in Problem Solving and the majority of that was now creative work. An increasing amount of creative work was being augmented.

This was the hospital where the Chief Financial Officer accidentally discovered 23 financial indicators over a nine-month period of time, as discussed earlier in the book. These 23 indicators showed the financial health of the hospital on a monthly basis.

To Do List

There was a dramatic change in the type of work being done between the first and second analyses. Remember that the WRM analysis also identifies a To Do list of items, gathered from the interviews. These are concepts and ideas that management considers of high importance. The list becomes the creative work opportunities that management prioritizes and uses to justify the hiring of new principals. Once new personnel are hired, these high-priority To Do's are assigned to them.

Conclusion

The hospital executives concluded that the number of meetings has gone down dramatically and remaining meetings are more productive. Support timeliness has improved with better communications. Delegation of work is occurring, to both principals and support personnel. The executives could use portable personal computers for home and business trips.

It is clear that management benefits from WRM if it is practiced on a regular basis. The majority of items from the first To Do list were accomplished in the first fourteen months. In addition, as the hospital became comfortable with the augmentation tools and the personal computer, the use of data resident in its host computer became pronounced.

A Computer Company's Marketing Department

Here is an example of a department that primarily performs activities that do not create revenues (known as "pacing" activities). WRM cleared the way for more time to be spent meeting customer requests, thus enhancing sales at the same time.

Background

A marketing organization of twenty-one salespeople was supported by one-half a support person, according to corporate standards, or one full-time support person for every forty-two salespeople. Could WRM help increase sales and, therefore, raise the productivity of the sales force?

Analysis

A common question posed by a potential customer is, "When can you have a proposal for me on this product?"

Remember, the sales support consisted of one-half of one person for twenty-one sales personnel and three managers. So, to answer the question, a good sales representative would have to consider available support, the demands of the business, the representative's needs against the needs of others in the sales office, and the point in the business cycle. In addition, the sales representative would have to make a priority analysis of other customer requests. It is quick mental gymnastics.

The salesperson thought for a minute and responded, "In three weeks." The answer given by the representative assumed that the majority of the work was routine. Not a difficult job at all. Now, let us suppose that management's objective was to better support the sales representatives and allow them to give a shorter response time. To accomplish this, management would have to add support personnel in two areas: first, off-load the sales representatives of routine work and, second, increase support of activities that provide customers with desired information more responsively. If the proposal can be offered in half the time, shouldn't that increase the number of possible buying decisions in a sales representative's territory?

We felt that if we made careful decisions about each activity in a sales representative's day, we could improve productivity by adding support personnel to accomplish the routine work. The process involved WRM as well as numerous sales office planning sessions. The salespeople were asked to identify the activities and applications that could be delegated to support personnel. The meetings were used to uncover additional activities that could be delegated. Under WRM, a sufficient volume of work was documented over a six-month period to justify hiring six additional support personnel. Nearly 30 percent of the sales force's time was freed of routine work and could be applied to increasing sales. It was management's hope that the sales personnel would use this free time in front of the customer. A suitable target might be to direct 70 to 75 percent of the freed-up time into activities that directly result in increased sales.

While WRM was well underway, the economy turned soft. In June of the following year, the average national sales office performance level dropped to 54 percent year-to-date attainment of national quota objectives. By then, management had already invested about eighteen months in WRM. In this soft economy, the local sales office's year-to-date quota attainment was 147 percent. It was the number 1 sales office in the country!

More Effective Management

Let us look at the management tactics that evolved from this experiment. Table II-3 shows the sales levels for highest and lowest performers. Remember that the before-WRM performance occurred in an up economy, while the after-WRM performance occurred in an economy that was slightly depressed.

Local management observed that when it creates an environment to maximize creative efforts, the spread between the lowest and highest performers is extreme. Before WRM, the spread was from 73 to 110 percent. After WRM, the spread was 98 to 368 percent. WRM had made it possible to dramatically increase the spread between the low and high

Table II-3. Sales performance.

| | Percent of Quota Achieved | |
	Before WRM	After WRM
# 21* Lowest-performing sales representative	73	98
# 20* Next to the lowest-ranked sales representative	75	99
# 19* Third lowest-ranked sales representative	76	123
# 1* Highest-ranked sales representative	110	368

*out of a total of 21 sales representatives

performers, proving once again that principals work to the level of the support they are provided and that limited support yields limited principal productivity.

Another interesting observation was that this sales office had only twenty-one representatives out of over 5,000 nationally, yet their performance was far better than average. The current national year-to-date average attainment for all sales representatives was 54 percent of quota. Of course, sales representatives do not compare themselves to national standards but rather to their peers in the same office.

For example, one day the third lowest sales representative was overheard talking to two senior managers from the headquarters location who were visiting the office. The visitors congratulated him on an outstanding year, but the representative said that he was having a terrible year! The visitors commented, "But the national average is only 54 percent." The sales representative said in rebuttal, "There are only two representatives below me, and in my opinion they do not belong in the business. That makes me the lowest rep in the branch office." It also demonstrates how peer pressure, rather than management pressure, will bring about improvement.

This example also illustrates why taking on more support personnel should *not* mean reducing the number of principals. There is the philosophy that a company should divide its sales force into thirds: top third, middle third, and bottom third. Some of the top third are promoted, some of the middle third move into the top or bottom, and the bottom either improve or are fired. We feel that philosophy is wrong, as this example shows.

When the support system was improved, even the two lowest performers were 99 percent and 98 percent of their annual quota! Should they have been fired? Remember, the national sales average was 54 percent. They were still better than national performance. Instead, peer pressure became the overpowering, motivating force. The two lowest performers eventually resigned, not from management pressure but from peer pressure through performance expectations. The productivity gap widened and became embarrassing for the low performers. A new standard had been established by the salespeople themselves. WRM is a much more productive and less stressful type of management. It regards people as excellent resources—mature, trustworthy employees.

This case answers another question, this time about Theory X and Theory Y. Does a company have to embrace one theory over the other? No. Both are applicable and both can be applied while providing respect to the individual.

In this sales example, the marketing people were driven by Theory Y. What about the technical professionals that install the equipment or the administrative people who do the paperwork? In this office, the administrative manager organized a task force, then used the four top performers to reorganize and match people and skills to jobs. Though the work was routine, he implemented an incentive system to reward administrative people. He used Theory X in a benevolent manner. Management openly said, "Thank you. Keep up the good work!" Theory X worked in the same environment as Theory Y.

Conclusion

This case shows that when routine work is diverted to support personnel, productivity increases. It also reinforces WRM as a means of pointing out poor performers and, through peer pressure, encouraging them to improve or leave.

A Brokerage Firm's Audit Department

This project demonstrates how WRM data are used in the five business functions: Access to Information, Problem Solving, Documentation Preparation and Processing, Distribution, and Communication. This Work Redistribution analysis was performed in the headquarters audit department of a stock brokerage firm.

Background

Each member of the internal audit department and all new hires had a master's degree. Most were fairly young and inexperienced. Auditing about ten departments a year, this department gave new hires the opportunity to learn many different facets of a complex business.

The typical audit itself was three weeks long. The first week was spent in the department being audited. The second week involved analyzing the data acquired during the first week. The third week was consumed with management presentations, first to the audit department managers to incorporate any changes, and then to the department in which the audit was done. Each auditor averaged ten audits a year along with some emergency audit requests. Since the latter were always ad hoc, they were disruptive to the department. An example of this disruptive work was the special quarterly audit of stock and bond certificates as well as other assets on hand. At the end of approximately eighteen months, the average auditor was then placed in a department in which he or she had developed an interest as a result of prior auditing experience.

Because of the department's training role, no auditor performed an audit on the same department twice before being promoted out of the department. This is significant because the audit process became static, and remained a manual process as a result.

Analysis

During WRM analysis, we discovered that auditors spent the following percentages of their total time in each of the five business functions:

Access to Information	1%
Problem Solving	27%
Document Preparation and Processing	18%
Distribution	4%
Communication	50%

Peter G. Sassone and A. Perry Schwartz, of Georgia Institute of Technology, say that there are two types of departments in the average business:[1] departments designed to support the internal process but which do not create any revenue, called paced work groups; and departments such as marketing, which have a direct impact on revenue or service, called pacing work groups. Generally, the greatest ROI is in a pacing department, thus these are the departments in which WRM is most critical. Would WRM benefit this department enough to justify its cost?

It was not obvious from the WRM data analysis if the auditors could be helped in any way. Problem Solving consumed 27 percent of the auditors' time and was performed during the second week of a three-week cycle, after gathering information from the departments visited. Fifty percent of the audit time was spent in Communication, which involved collecting information through interviews the first week and presenting the findings to management the third week. Document Preparation and Processing was used to prepare materials for the management of the department being audited, as well as the manager of the audit department. Once the presentations were concluded, a final report was generated.

During the WRM interview process, we explored the time spent in Problem Solving and Communication. In order to better understand the work, the time spent in each business function was separated into routine and creative work, shown in Table II-4.

One of the mysteries was why only 1 percent of the time was spent on Access to Information. How did they prepare

Table II-4. Distribution of principals' time (percentage of total time).

	Routine Work	Creative Work	Total
Access to Information	1	–	1
Problem Solving	19	8	27
Document Preparation and Processing	4	14	18
Distribution	2	2	4
Communication	26	24	50
	52	48	100

for an audit? We asked why so little time was spent in this function and discovered that the auditors were unaware of the fact that much of the information they needed already existed on the computer. Since most of the auditors were new, they did not know enough about the company and its data processing systems. Also, the company did not have the data in a relational database, where they were easily accessible. Lastly, the auditors were not sufficiently trained to access the information. In fact, the auditors did not have enough experience in auditing even to be concerned that there might be a way to conduct an audit other than a face-to-face visit.

We started to realize why so much time was spent in Communication. The auditors had to recapture all the information already on computer (routine information), as well as the new information that was applicable (creative information), through face-to-face interviews. After realizing where the opportunities for augmentation existed, the auditors described the audit process. After an initial WRM analysis, we spent some time with the data processing department. The auditors learned which 50 to 70 percent of the data needed already was in the main computer system and how it could be made available through a relational database. It then became obvious that only new data required face-to-face communication. Since the auditors never did a second audit on the same department, queries against a relational database had never come up, even with the more experienced auditors.

The preparation of audit material for department review as well as audit management review represented a first-time event. As a result, it was easy to understand why preparations for the reviews were a creative experience, even though the process was quite routine.

Increased Time

As a result of WRM analysis and our recommendations, the auditors reviewed the department data that could be accessed for a pre-audit. The auditors prepared two documents. The first listed the data to be placed in a relational database; the second was an estimate of how much time could be saved using a relational database to accomplish a pre-audit. The auditors also agreed that if they were able to accomplish a second audit on a department, their estimates could be significantly reduced as additional experience was gained. Table II-5 shows the findings, with a 47 percent saving in time.

The executives of this brokerage firm received several options as to how to use the additional professional resources freed up as a consequence of WRM analysis:

- Have auditors accomplish more audits of the same depth, and improve their productivity from ten audits to almost fifteen per year.
- Have auditors complete the same number of audits in 47 percent less time.
- Have auditors increase the technical depth of the audits or perform more audits in sensitive departments.

There was yet another alternative. Like many others, this brokerage firm was purchasing stocks and bonds and keeping them on hand for the investors. The quantity of negotiable documents had increased to a point where the audit department had been asked to hire two additional auditors just to manage and audit these negotiable documents. While we generally agree with Sassone and Schwartz in their use of paced and pacing departments as a basis for

Table II-5. Time estimates for audit activities (in days).

	Department Activities	Auditor's Analysis	Findings/ Presentations	Total
Current	5	5	5	15
Proposed	2	3	3	8
Savings	3	2	2	7

prioritizing department studies, this example may be an exception to the rule. The brokerage firm discovered several millions of dollars were at risk with the inventory of negotiable assets.

With the 47 percent increase in the auditors' time, the department took on the audit of negotiable documents without hiring the additional auditors. Though most consultants would say that paced departments do not offer the financial savings a pacing department does, the direct benefits in this case were measurable. With better audits and better control of assets, the liability of the firm is greatly reduced. Seen in the light of potential lawsuits, a paced department may be equal in value to a pacing department, and WRM analysis can be of substantial value. For this firm, there is no question that the benefits were real.

Conclusion

This case illustrates an important point about WRM analysis. Data obtained through the work diaries gain their full meaning when matched with interviews of the people in the work group. The interview showed that the auditors' work could be augmented—this time merely by making available to the auditors data already in existence. The case also points to the need for training in the use of augmentation tools.

A Nuclear Engineering Company

This project involved the headquarters staff of 200 people at a nuclear reactor company. Using Work Redistribution Management, we established criteria to assess productivity changes.

Background

We quickly found that this engineering firm had the following relationship of people to product, and that this relationship was the standard for gauging productivity:

100 principals + 10 support personnel = 10 nuclear contracts/ year

The company had a straightforward ratio of people to contracts: Ten engineers and one support person could produce one contract a year. In other words, management viewed the ratio of principals to support personnel and the number of contracts produced as a *fixed* relationship.

The engineering company was planning to expand in order to handle fifteen contracts a year. Since management had a fixed view of productivity, it also considered the cost of growth as fixed. Management's logic was straightforward: If 100 engineers produce 10 contracts a year, then 150 engineers will produce 15 contracts a year; if it takes 10 people to support 100 engineers, it takes 15 support people to support 150 engineers. This is a common management assumption. In some businesses, this logic leads managers to believe that all work is routine, and that it is all viable for automation. As the work becomes automated, the cost of information technology is justified through a reduction in support personnel.

The implications of excessive management growth are easy to predict using this rigid view of work. In this case, the productivity objective was five additional contracts, which meant hiring fifty additional engineers and five more support people. Management had a fixed budget forecast and the company was satisfied:

> 50 engineers @ $50,000   = $2,500,000
> 5 support people @ $20,000   = $ 100,000

Our supposition was that a *variable* relationship exists between people and production. That is, ten principals might be able to produce more than one contract a year if augmentation tools were available.

With its budget in mind, the company agreed to a simple experiment: Keep the number of principals at 100. If our assumptions about work were true, WRM analysis would uncover routine work that could be delegated to support people. Would WRM analysis also prove that it was better to hire additional support personnel to perform the newly delegated routine work? We did not know the answer to that question at this stage.

Analysis

Under our approach, the company began performing a logical transfer of routine work from a $50,000-a-year principal to a $20,000-a-year support person. That made good business sense to the executives. As an engineer's time was freed up, the engineer was allowed to perform more creative work required to produce the current contracts as well as the incremental five new contracts.

The two-hour recall diary was used to identify which work was routine and which was creative. Potential new activities and applications were also highlighted. Then the work was redistributed and the right equipment was provided to perform each job.

The impact of new augmentation software tools would be apparent in our follow-up WRM analysis. (In the end, this company found so many activities and applications to delegate to support personnel, it decided to perform WRM analysis every six months.) Work Redistribution Management took into account the company's costs for people, equipment, and organizational changes required to redistribute the work. The additional costs of technology, along with the additional costs of support personnel, would be compared to the original cost estimates of hiring fifty principals ($2.5 million) and five additional support people ($100,000).

Understand that the justification for WRM came after the fact. Because it is a first-time effort, creative work can only be evaluated after the ideas have been accepted and implemented. On the other hand, justification to invest in technology for routine work can be calculated before the fact. This is a critical difference between traditional automation and augmentation. This company did not object to trying a new organizational structure before justification was proved. Their reasoning was understandable. If support personnel could handle the activities and applications principals were currently performing, delegation made sense. Management had allowed routine work to back up onto the principals' desks, restricting their productivity. The results are shown in Figure II-1.

One year later, three costs were recalculated: (1) the cost of additional support personnel to accomplish delegated routine work; (2) the cost of new equipment (technology); and (3) the cost of additional principals with special or critical skills. These costs were compared to the original budget and the value of the new contracts produced.

What did management learn? First, the relationship of principals to support is not fixed; it is variable, depending on the type of work being accomplished. Second, augmentation tools increase the productivity of principals. Third, management must get the right work to the right employee. Fourth, work is dynamically changing; what is creative today will be routine tomorrow. Fifth, there is a variable relationship between people and productivity; when principals have augmentation tools for creative work, their productivity increases. Sixth, people need the right equipment to do their job; word processing and data processing technology is viable for routine work, but creative work needs personal computers and augmentation tools.

The savings of $840,000 a year were almost incidental

Figure II-1. Comparison of costs.

	Traditional Approach		WRM Approach	
	People	Cost	People	Cost
Principals (current)	100	$5,000,000	100	$5,000,000
Support (current)	10	$ 200,000	10	$ 200,000
Recommendations:				
Additional Principals	50	$2,500,000	-	-
Additional Support	5	$ 100,000	13	$ 260,000
Augmentation Technology	-	-	-	$1,500,000
	165	$7,800,000	123	$6,960,000
Total Net Savings per Year		$ 840,000		
Contracts per Year		10		15
Cost per Contract		$ 780,000		$ 464,000
Net Savings per Contract		$ 316,000		

to the changes in management philosophy. Organizational structure was changed to allow WRM analysis and delegation of work to continue on a periodic basis.

Productivity

This company was already processing ten contracts a year. It had a list of the required documents needed to produce a nuclear contract. As a result, management asked if it were possible to track documents by contract and type of worker. We worked out a system to accomplish this objective.

The results of this project were very interesting. For example, there was a change in the number and type of documents produced when the WRM system was introduced. Initially, the company routinely processed about 2,200 lines of text work per day. A year later, volume had risen to 6,395 lines of information per day, an increase of 191 percent.

The composition of work dramatically differed as well:

	% Before WRM (2,200 Lines)	% After WRM (6,395 Lines)
Routine work	85	44
Reactive work	12	29
Creative work	3	27

In the original system, engineers obviously worked to the level of support provided. The system was only capable of handling routine work. In addition, the original system did not support the creative work the engineers needed to perform. The new system changed the way principals worked and were supported. As a result, their volume increased drastically, with 56 percent of that increase in the two categories of reactive and creative work.

Each principal in the study was tracked anonymously.

An illustration of documentation produced by one engineer is shown in Figure II-2.

The old saying is apropos: It is not what you expect, but what you inspect that is important. The WRM system gave management the ability to inspect the type of work being done, not to inspect the *individual*. The company found that managing the good performer paid higher dividends than managing the poor performer.

Figure II-2. Engineer 35 before and after productivity study.

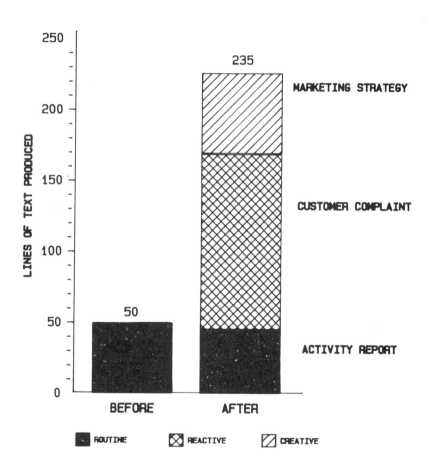

Customer Responsiveness

One of the company's concerns was customer responsiveness. Documentation was a key aspect of customer service, so management asked if we could expedite the preparation and processing of customer documents. Document
tracking *compares* the total lines of information the system
can support for each activity or application to the revenue
generated from the applications. A comparison was made
between the original system and the WRM system. WRM
analysis showed a relationship among three factors: (1) system demand (principals' demand for creation), (2) system
output (support's ability to produce demand), and (3) system
backlog (work backlog).

Figure II-3 shows these three conditions for a period of
ten days before implementation of the WRM recommendations.

During the initial review of the workload, the lines of
documentation averaged just over 2,100 per day. This was
prior to the new WRM system being installed. Management
discovered that there was one major workload peak during

Figure II-3. First WRM analysis.

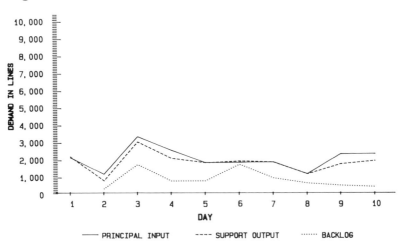

this period, on day 3, with a second peak about day 10. This peaking of demand was termed "Task Completion Syndrome," defined as the number of days it took to complete a single stage of document preparation—that is, draft cycle, revision cycle, final copy, and so on. The engineers believed that the quicker the preparation cycle, the quicker the document could be delivered to the customer, but the more extensive the preparation cycle, the more accurate the document. Document preparation and production time in a competitive industry is vitally important.

The second WRM analysis was done ninety days later. By this time, a number of support personnel had been added, as well as augmentation tools. The second analysis revealed a significant increase in the number of Task Completion Syndromes during a similar ten-day period, as shown in Figure II-4.

There were two significant findings: (1) the visible change in the quantity of work being completed and (2) three Task Completion Syndromes occurring in the same ten-day period, whereas only one occurred before. Why? WRM gave the answers.

One of the most logical explanations for increased vol-

Figure II-4. Second WRM analysis.

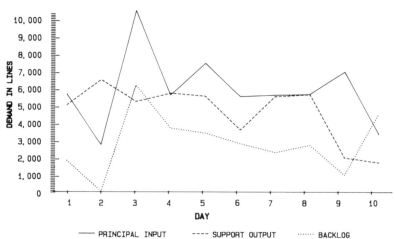

ume is that the first period was a slow work time and the second a peak time. This might have been true if the company had not reached its goals, but it had.

No, the difference had to do with a visible change in the quantity of work completed. In other words, the engineers tended to work to the level of support they received. If a company increases support, it increases productivity as well.

This company understood the human limitations described in Appendix A of this book, but its goal was to overcome these limitations by augmenting the engineers' activities and modifying its support system to decrease the turnaround time. In studying Figure II-4, we noticed that between day 1 and day 2, engineers were engaged in routine work: (1) Principal input went down, (2) support output went up, and (3) backlog went down. The principal's input was low because he or she spent less time giving routine instructions for routine information to be sent to a client. Routine information was usually already created and stored on a word processor; all the principal had to do was identify the document number and provide the few variables to customize the document. Support output went up when use of these stored documents went up, because word processing produced customized documents at the rate of 180 wpm. The backlog went down when support kept up with the input and caught up with the backlog from previous days. In contrast, between day 2 and day 3, principal input went up, support output went down, and backlog went up. Therefore, during these two days, engineers were engaged in creative work. The principal spent a great deal of time originating a high volume of new work. The new work placed a peak demand on the support system, which could accomplish new work at only 60 wpm, therefore, the backlog increased.

Another piece of intelligence comes from the height of the lines in these graphs. In Figure II-3, all three lines are below a 5,000-line volume for the ten-day period. Look at day 3. Principal input rose to about 4,500 lines. In Figure II-4, principal input for day 3 rose to 11,000 lines of information. The difference between 4,500 and 11,000 is 6,500 additional lines of information, made possible because of added support personnel.

The graphs, along with the accompanying interviews, suggested that:

1. Principals could be more thorough in document preparation.
2. A potential for higher-quality finished products existed.
3. There was a tremendous opportunity for change (revision) and precision.

The other significant finding from the second WRM analysis was the increase in Task Completion Syndromes. As mentioned earlier, three syndromes occurred in the same ten-day period whereas only one had occurred before WRM. This was because the cycle was shortened. The shortening of the production cycle was a big factor in decreasing the customer's decision time by getting the documents to the customer sooner. This allowed more customer decisions to occur in any given period, through quicker responsiveness and delivery of decision-making documentation. The result: One hundred engineers went from producing ten contracts a year to 15.5 contracts a year.

Conclusion

The tracking of documents in this case demonstrated that the engineers were working to their level of support. As support increased, the same number of engineers produced 5.5 additional contracts. This company was now convinced that principals work to the level of support provided. Management learned that if it increases support, it increases productivity. The company also learned never to decrease support personnel to pay for technology. By measuring the production of principals before and after, management was able to continually get the right job to the right person. This is not possible when the number of support personnel is reduced. When the WRM analysis was begun, the support ratio was 10:1. After one year, the ratio was 4:1, and 15.5 contracts were produced annually.

A Computer Company's Advertising Department

This project involved several departments whose responsibilities included the coordination and announcement of new products. It illustrates the need for getting the right job to the right person, and also for having proper standardized augmentation tools.

Background

The advertising department had twenty principals, two of whom were managers. There also were two administrative support people. The company wanted greater efficiency and productivity in this important department.

Analysis

We began by evaluating the work of the principals in the department. Table II-6 represents their typical workday.

Table II-6. Distribution of principals' time (percentage of total time).

	Routine Work	Creative Work	Total
Access to Information	.5	.5	1
Problem Solving	6	6	12
Document Preparation and Processing	15	13	28
Distribution	10	2	12
Communication	23	24	47
	54.5	45.5	100

During the interview process, the principals were asked how frequently they used support personnel and for what type of assistance. The following shows their answers for each of five support activities:

	Number of Principals Using Support Activity
Mail	20
Typing	3
Federal Express	4
Copying	1
Making reservations	2

In short, very little support was provided by the administrative structure. During the interview process, the support personnel were questioned as to whom they supported and they replied, "The managers," indicating they did not have time to support non-management principals. Yet when interviewed, the managers assumed that staff professionals were receiving the same level of support. There was a misunderstanding about the function of the support persons and how much work they could handle.

A prime illustration of work activities out of balance was that principals retrieved all their mail from a central filing drawer instead of having it distributed to them twice a day. Typing support was also weak. Management felt that typing could be done by principals through word processing software on their personal computers if they required anything typed. Once again the implicit assumption that all work is routine was evident.

Only four principals received Federal Express assistance, yet all used Federal Express. In fact, WRM analysis revealed that 12 percent of the principals' time was spent on Distribution and the majority of this was Federal Express. Twelve percent of 20 principals' time equals 2.4 man-years at $50,000 per year, spent preparing, picking up, and delivering Federal Express packages. A minimum of 70 percent of this time could be delegated to support personnel at an annual salary of $20,000 per year. Seventy percent times 2.4 man-years equals 1.7 man-years; 1.7 multiplied by $50,000 equals $85,000 a year. If support personnel accomplished this work, the cost would be only $34,000 a year.

Augmentation tools were not standardized, which inhibited delegation of work and effective communication. For example, the department generated a product announcement package which was a collection of documents from seven other departments. The contributing documents were an initial planning guide, a market support plan, and a request for announcing the product. The remaining contents of the package consisted of input from other areas such as direct response marketing, advertising, and direct marketing, plus the press requirements.

The department could have copied selected sections of the documents to insert into the package *if* the contributing departments had compatible software. However, they did not! The documents had to be retyped once they arrived in the advertising department.

The advertising department used two different text software packages. All twenty-two employees had intelligent workstations, but only nine used them for word processing. Of these nine, six had Software A and three had Software B. Of the six with Software A, two were support personnel. Of the four principals who had Software A, two used it and two did not because they had *never been trained* on it.

Standardization

In this company, as in most, software standards have rarely been set or are generally ignored if they do exist. Compatibility between software products is difficult at best. It certainly does not exist where each individual or department manager has the ability to set standards. Software standards must be established on a corporate-wide basis or the proper redistribution of work is restricted and the cost of self-training exorbitant.

The same was true for spreadsheet activities. The majority of principals in the department performed repetitive, routine manipulation of data with the use of calculators. In fact, 57 percent of all calculations were manual. Why? There was no training! A spreadsheet program can be difficult to learn without some assistance. Aside from that, of the four people using spreadsheets, three of their programs were the same and one was not. If a corporate standard had been set, compatibility and integration of information from one program to another would have been achieved, reducing the repetitive recapturing of information. This work group shared information with three sister organizations in other parts of the country. Each of the work groups was trying to set up its own financial tracking system for budgets. Each was using a different, non-compatible spreadsheet program and could not share the information electronically. We recommended standardization to eliminate these problems.

Training

The WRM analysis revealed that the majority of intelligent workstations were being used only for electronic mail. If this was their only usage, dumb terminals should be used because they are cheaper. But the real problem was a lack of training on the augmentation tools themselves.

Some companies feel it is the end users' responsibility to train themselves and retrain themselves every time software is changed. The result is half-hearted attempts at training, with the majority of people rejecting software programs. Query, spreadsheet, graphics, and text editor programs are as different as night and day. The skills required for software package "A" are not transferable to software package "B." Therefore, setting corporate standards also eases training needs.

Work Redistribution

The analysis showed that the principal-to-support ratio was 10:1. The company's management strategy was to increase this ratio to 15:1. Like most companies, it viewed all work as routine. Consequently, the goal was to decrease support and increase the number of principals. However, WRM revealed the flaw in this thinking. We defined the activities and applications with volume at the support level and got this work to a word or data processing center. This move gave the support personnel time to take on additional activities delegated by the principals. We had to be sensitive to two aspects of delegating work. First, businesses have been lowering the skill and performance requirements of support personnel over the past ten to fifteen years, simply by expecting them to accomplish only routine work. In this department, support personnel spent 99 percent of their time on routine activities. Second, support personnel have only been asked to perform independent activities such as typing, filing, making reservations or appointments, and so on, and are not used to accomplishing a complete business process.

We suggested that future support personnel be capable of accepting the delegation of entire business processes, as opposed to isolated activities. For example, an experienced support person could consolidate all seven documents of that announcement package into at least the rough draft. Then, the support person could work with the principal to finalize the document and ultimately assume most of the responsibility for it.

Conclusion

Jobs will change dramatically in the future, as corporations and public institutions accelerate their restructuring and downsizing. The work of support will change the quickest, as the WRM process becomes an accepted part of business life. Work Redistribution Management will enhance the work of both the support personnel and principals because it will provide them with dynamic, creative challenges.

A Manufacturing Company's Costing Department

A manufacturer of athletic goods had a group of principals responsible for determining the cost of goods manufactured. They accomplished this by using a thick cost book printed by the data processing department once a month, which contained the cost of materials used to produce the products. This was an interesting use of Work Redistribution Management because it concerned a department whose work was highly routine.

Background

The principals in this work group tracked all the materials required to produce a product through the manufacturing cycle: raw materials, decals, buttons, cord for ties, thread, zippers, and numerous other inventory items. After tracking the quantity and specifications of the goods used in the manufacturing process, the work group looked up the prices of all materials in the computer-produced book of inventory items. The principals used literally a manual spreadsheet format. They entered the variables after finding the data in the price book. With a calculator, the total cost of goods was figured line by line. Was there a way to increase productivity?

Analysis

WRM analysis was performed in this group of eighteen people—eleven principals and seven support personnel. While virtually all the activities were repetitive, they were accomplished manually. The growth of the business was excellent and pressure to produce goods had prevented management from taking the time to automate this portion of the business. Table II-7 is a profile of how the principals spent their time.

Problem Solving took a great deal of time and consisted of a number of activities, one of which was termed work with data. In WRM analysis we asked the employees what techniques or products were used to assist them in working with data.

Several choices were available, such as a personal computer, a calculator, or other devices. Working with data took

Table II-7. Distribution of principals' time (percentage of total time).

	Routine Work	Creative Work	Total
Access to Information	1	–	1
Problem Solving	43	19	62
Document Preparation and Processing	2	1	3
Distribution	5	3	8
Communication	18	8	26
	69	31	100

216 hours a week: 31 of these were spent using a personal computer while 185 were with a calculator or manually using longhand.

The principals indicated that 85 percent of the 185 hours was a lengthy routine process with low volume, where the personal computer and augmentation tools could be helpful. However, day-to-day business pressures were stopping management from augmenting its employees' activities and improving their productivity.

WRM analysis also showed that support personnel spent 174 hours (81 percent of their total hours) working with data; 91 percent of the work was routine. In the case of principals as well as support personnel, only 1 percent of their workdays was spent accessing information. The data were in the computer, but there was no way for the end users to access it.

The cost in employee hours of manually looking up information and then manipulating it with a calculator was costing the business millions of dollars in lost productivity, simply because it did not have electronic access to existing data, nor the ability to download data to personal computers.

Automation and Delegation

The solution was to both automate and augment the process and then delegate much of the work. This was accomplished by building a relational database with all the pricing information and giving workers direct access to data. This process also permitted material reference numbers (for the items used to manufacture a set of goods) to be entered into a spreadsheet. The computer filled in the name and prices, and downloaded them into the spreadsheet. The resulting calculation was the cost of the goods sold.

This method was more accurate and took less time because it was already in machine-readable form. The data were entered only once, and could be transmitted to other departments of inventory, billing, and cost analysis. The first time a set of costing computations was set up, it required the skill and knowledge of a principal. However, the subsequent use of this spreadsheet for a particular product could be delegated to a support person to perform.

The productivity benefits would enable the company to reduce the number of professionals in the costing department by 38 percent if the volume and types of goods produced were relatively constant. Was the production of goods being constrained by the costing department? The answer was no, however, the costing department was previously understaffed and worked an unusual amount of overtime. The manufacturing facility was located in a remote location and needed principals with similar skills, but attracting loyal, qualified help in its remote location was always a problem. By increasing the costing department's productivity and reducing overtime, the entire operation benefitted. Surplus principals were transferred to other jobs at this manufacturing facility.

Conclusion

The most interesting aspect of this case was the finding that WRM works well for routine work as well as creative. When the work is highly routine, there is a chance to free up personnel who could be used more productively in other areas.

A Petroleum Company

This project involved a petroleum company and its accounts receivable. Work Redistribution Management showed that work is dynamic, not static, and that the correct mix of people yields the most creative work. Yet reluctance to invest in technology and training kept the business operation in the Dark Ages.

Background

Principals in this company were receiving salaries in the range of $65,000 to $75,000 a year. Yet much of their time was spent on routine activities. These routine activities consisted of reviewing accounts receivable by manually comparing two different computer reports—one showing debits and the other showing credits. The company wanted to know if there was a better, more cost-effective way of determining who owed the company money, and whether costs to correct that situation would be justified.

There were 263 customer accounts (526 reports) that had to be reconciled each month, yet "end users" had no direct access to data. Five years earlier, the data processing reports and system were put in place, but not enhanced much since then. The tracking and reconciliation problem had evolved since then. In short, the department's user needs had changed but the automated process had not.

Over twenty-seven principals performed the accounts receivable activity. Eight were "temporaries" hired for "90 days" (to keep up with the volume) *eighteen months ago*! This showed that the work had changed, but management had not kept up with that change.

The average account had an outstanding value of $2 million. Reconciliation took two days per account each month. Improvements meant changes to the system, the people, and the equipment. The productivity of the people could now be measured, and the cost of those changes could be compared to improvements in productivity.

Analysis

WRM analysis showed that 76 percent of the principals' activity was routine work. The first part of the reconciliation process activity was a manual check to see if missing debits and credits showed up on the reports. This was a process a computer could perform more efficiently. If checking with other members of the department did not show matching credits, then a *manual* tracking process was used which involved contacting the company to see if payments had been made, when, and for what amount. The invoice number was then checked against the payment made and the location to which the remittance was sent.

The tracking and collection aspects were the portion of the job that the company categorized as creative. This is what the people were hired to do, but they were only spending 10 to 15 percent of their time on this process; the rest of their work was best suited for automation.

A yearly WRM review would save this company a tremendous amount of money, since it literally had over 200 people performing this job manually. Yet management indicated it could not afford to evaluate work once a year. Now, some readers may be shocked that such a basic business process could have grown to the point where hundreds of people were involved. It is such a simple, straightforward process to automate, perfect for traditional data processing. There must be a reason why it was not automated, right? Well, this was 1987. It existed because management assumed that work is static, and failed to reanalyze the work, the equipment needed, and the procedures necessary to improve the dynamically changing process, an assumption of which we are all guilty.

There were two major opportunities. The first was to move much of the debit and credit reconciliation into the computer and write an automated application to replace the manual reconciliation. The remainder of the reconciliation process, then, would be better done by support personnel as opposed to principals.

The second opportunity was to correct the mix of people. For example, there were twenty-seven principals in the department and only 15 percent of their time was spent performing the work for which they were hired. In essence, twenty-seven principals were partly doing the high-value work that four full-time principals could perform. The potential savings in salaries was as high as $1,150,000 a year.

The first reduction could have been to release the eight temporaries, with no long-term consequences to the company. The next fifteen employees would have been another matter. The company was looking for new people for another division. Here were fifteen loyal employees ready to move to a new opportunity, welcoming more challenging work.

A major portion of the cost justification for augmentation equipment to help the remaining principals and support personnel perform the activities and applications could have been provided by the salary savings of the eight "temporary" people released. Additional cost justification could have come from two additional sources: the additional fifteen full-time employees no longer required in the department, and the value of money in terms of quicker collection and earlier investment. Since this department dealt with accounts receivable, any improvements would increase the department's ability to collect millions of dollars faster.

Conclusion

Since creative work is a company's future, freeing up more time for principals to spend on creative activities provides a tremendous edge on competitors. Remember, changes made to routine work can be determined ahead of time, however, justification for augmenting creative work must be documented in the future, once the value of the new work is determined. This takes some patience and a great deal of corporate vision.

Appendixes

Appendix A

Technology and the Human Brain: Information Systems for Office Operations

Understanding the nature of people and how they work is basic to developing a new organizational office support system. The human being is a marvelously complex and wonderful creature. In a simplistic sense, we can think of the human brain as the central processing unit of a computer. The part of the brain that is most important for work is the short-term memory. The short-term memory helps us assimilate new information. It can process thoughts at speeds of 1,000 to 1,200 words per minute (wpm). That is fast.

Thinking is not enough. We must have a way to record our thoughts. At present there are only three ways: (1) to write the information at 10 to 25 words per minute; (2) to type the information at 25 to 100 words per minute; or (3) to dictate the information at 150 to 300 words per minute.

If dictation is the fastest way to record thoughts, why do most business people refuse to use dictation equipment? Because we want to see these thoughts on paper immediately.

Very few businesses provide a rapid turnaround time for hard copy of a draft, whether dictated or not. Instead, most offer an eight-hour turnaround time, some perhaps only four hours. Of course, some people will immediately respond that they use dictation equipment and that it suits their work perfectly. These respondents typically are second- or third-level managers and most of their dictation is simple for them to accomplish, so it does not require a rapid turnaround time.

Another factor in the successful use of dictation is the accessibility of secretarial support. In most businesses today only managers have direct access to secretarial help. Professional staff generally do not have a secretary to take dictation or transcribe material.

As we have seen, work spans a continuum of difficulty, from very simple or routine to very complex or creative. Why did we not use "simple" and "complex" to describe routine and creative work? Because the terms imply a range of difficulty that varies with the performer, depending on experience and skills. Just as work spans a continuum, so does our allowance for turnaround time. When work is simple, we can tolerate a longer turnaround time. When it is more complex, we want a shorter turnaround time.

Short-term Memory

Let us use some exercises to illustrate the role short-term memory has in performing simple and complex activities. First, ask a group of friends or colleagues to give you the name of the most famous or most well-known American president. The response will probably be one of four: George Washington, Abraham Lincoln, John F. Kennedy, or the current president.

Let us assume Lincoln is the consensus of the group. Consider "Lincoln" as a piece of routine information. Now, ask one of your friends to use only his or her short-term memory (no pad or pencil) to listen to you read the names of some presidents in random order. (This assumes your friend has not memorized all the presidents or has no unusual ability to memorize lists, which has happened to us once.) The remainder of the group may use whatever tools are at hand, probably a pad and pencil.

Then read the following six names in order:

1. Van Buren
2. Taylor
3. Harrison
4. Buchanan
5. Polk
6. Hayes

Ask your friend to repeat the names back to you immediately. The average person's response will be to give three or four names; occasionally, someone will repeat five. Now ask one of the other members of the group to repeat the names. He or she will repeat all six.

Why can the average person using only his or her short-term memory only recall three or four names? Because there is a basic human limitation to our short-term memory. While it works very fast, its capacity for remembering new information is limited to 3–5 new variables at a time.

Now, read the following names to your friend:

1. Van Buren
2. Harrison
3. Polk
4. Taylor
5. Buchanan
6. Hayes
7. Tyler
8. Fillmore
9. Pierce
10. Johnson
11. Grant
12. Garfield

Ask your friend to repeat as many as possible. Normally, the response is four or five names, but it is not uncommon to receive only the same number as before. Sometimes the individual repeats fewer names, which happens when the short-term memory's ability to cope with the number of variables is exceeded and frustration results. In short, without the ability to record information instantly, the average person's short-term memory is limited to approximately four variables. Again, ask any other member of the group to repeat the names. That person will give you all twelve names.

When a variable—or, in the case of work, an activity—is inputted repeatedly, it is committed to our long-term memory and bypasses the storage limitation of our short-term memory. Our long-term memory has less restrictive storage limits. Consider for a moment your ability to memorize phone numbers, song lyrics, names, addresses, directions, formulas, foreign languages, and so on. These use your long-term memory.

In business, routine situations have few variables. The work is simple because the information needed has previously been committed to memory. Performance of routine work is not inhibited by our short-term memory. Creative work requires comprehension, retention, and evaluation, which involve more than four variables. Traditional office support systems have frustrated employees doing creative work because generally they have not been designed to augment complex or creative activities. They have not provided that rapid turnaround time we mentioned earlier.

Rapid Turnaround

Why do most people doing creative work become frustrated when there is more than a thirty-minute turnaround time? The best response we can give is one that has withstood the test of time. If you write longhand for 30 minutes, you will fill one standard typewritten page. Once the thoughts are written, we can see the results. We are able to analyze them and revise them. It is usually easier to write something in longhand than to wait more than thirty minutes for a draft.

There is another important element. When we draft our ideas, we perform an essential step in the creative process. We think, rethink, and use our short-term memory. For the creative work process to be most productive, we need a turnaround time of less than thirty minutes. This simple concept is not understood or supported in most businesses.

Rapid turnaround to augment creative work represents a new design point for office support systems. The larger the number of variables in a complex problem, the faster the turnaround required. This need is not met by traditional dictation systems and is the primary reason why dictation equipment is rarely used by non-management principals. Since dictation equipment fails us in the non-management portion of our business development, we assume it will not support us in the management and executive portions of our careers as well. This is not true, for as we are promoted, we use creative abilities to make decisions and evaluations on the creative output of our professional staff. More of our work is routine and can be dictated.

Let us consider a "what if" situation. What if you had a personal computer that had a microphone attached? As quickly as you spoke into the microphone, let's assume the words appeared on the screen. Once the words were on the screen, you could make revisions just by placing the cursor where you wanted the new words. Would you dictate all your thoughts into the computer and be free of longhand, short-hand, and keyboarding forever? Virtually everyone responds yes. Speech is by far the fastest way to transfer information from our short-term memory into a revisable form.

Ideally, this is the most productive way to record our thoughts. The speed of speech—150 to 300 wpm—is closest to the speed of our thought process. Unfortunately, there is no speech recognition system generally available yet to take verbal input and display it on a screen. A principal speaks at 300 wpm normally and slows to 150 wpm for dictation. A good transcriptionist types at 60 to 80 wpm. Therefore, it takes up to three transcriptionists to keep up with a principal's dictation using today's technology.

The second-best method of capturing creative work is by directly keying in the information. The capture rate for keying is 30 to 60 wpm. Most older principals (40+ years) do not know how to type well; this work is generally accomplished by support personnel. If typing is part of the document preparation phase of the creative process, then typing can augment a principal's ability to do creative work.

Since voice recognition technology is an invention waiting to arrive, keyboarding offers an interim solution, even though it has its limitations. Of course, the majority of younger-generation principals are keyboard trained. *All* future generations must be keyboard trained if they are to be successful.

The least productive method of capturing creative efforts is longhand. Longhand averages only 15 wpm, yet it is the method most widely used in the business world today. A significant limitation of longhand, as well as keyboarding, is the inability of our brain to retain new variables when some are diverted to following the rules of grammar, spelling, and memorization of the keyboard. Many people also attempt to prioritize information while writing down their thoughts, which also consumes a portion of their mental capacity.

Memorization

Let us return to the presidential names exercise. Read the following nine names in sequence to your friend and once again have your friend feed them back:

1. Bush
2. Reagan
3. Carter
4. Ford
5. Nixon

6. Johnson
7. Kennedy
8. Eisenhower
9. Truman

This time your friend remembered seven or eight names. Why the difference? Most people remember all but one of the presidents, especially if they are over 25 years old. These presidents were in office during their lifetime, so their names are committed to long-term memory, almost by osmosis through the repetition of TV, radio, magazines, and newspapers. The names are easy to remember, and, as a result, they are not impacted by the limitations of short-term memory.

The same is true in business. If a sequence of activities is experienced or happens repetitively, it is memorized. Routine work can still have multiple variables, but the variables are memorized over time. The limitations of short-term memory are applicable only the first time someone attempts to learn something new.

Of course, what is routine for one company or individual may be new for another. For that reason, it is crucial that companies classify their own work, not have it done by vendors or consultants. When training new employees or presenting new procedures to current employees, management must recognize that the human mind can only handle three to five new variables at a time (within a few minutes).

The Human Limitations in Creative Work

Creative work is not so simple as storing three or four items in short-term memory. Principals utilize processes like prioritization, which complicates matters.

To illustrate human shortcomings when it comes to prioritization, let's return to the presidential names exercise. Read the following names to your friend in sequence:

1. Van Buren
2. Harrison
3. Polk
4. Taylor
5. Buchanan
6. Hayes
7. Tyler
8. Fillmore
9. Pierce
10. Johnson
11. Grant
12. Garfield

Now ask your friend to prioritize the presidents by one of the following: age, demographics, chronological order, number of terms, or political party. Unless he or she is a master of American history, you'll get no response and be asked to repeat the information three or four times. Many people fail to capture the names before a prioritization challenge, and their short-term memory becomes even more cluttered.

If someone asks you to name the vowels in alphabetical order, do you have to stop and think? That's probably the first time someone mentioned alphabetical order in relation to the vowels. But an instant of creative problem solving helped you recall that you originally learned the vowels in alphabetical order, so the answer comes quickly. But next time, suppose you're asked to give the vowels in reverse order. This causes you to transfer the vowels from long-term memory to short-term memory and then to manipulate them. Your verbalized response probably takes longer, because you're busy rearranging the data. Yet this is a common business operation, especially in creative situations.

Systems used in a business must be designed with an understanding of the limitations of the human brain, as well as of the different types of work people perform. The proper office technology tools can neutralize human limitations and augment productivity. Yet in most businesses, "office systems" are still aimed at routine-oriented work. The integrated technology still missing from the office is that which helps principals deal with multiple variables in the creative process. They need to be able to access information, manipulate the information easily, and document their thoughts and ideas quickly.

Appendix B

The Work Redistribution Management Activity Diary: Additional Information on Completing the Entries

The two-hour recall diary is described in Chapter 7, and a complete copy is included as Appendix C. The first three pages of the diary contain general instructions for completing the entries, however, sometimes there are additional questions. This material covers the commonly asked questions.

In-Person Meetings

You can break any period of time into more than one classification. You should designate an activity as routine, reactive-routine, reactive-creative, or creative. Let's assume that you had a one-hour meeting. On the two-hour activity log, put the 60 minutes in the time column.

Activity	Application	Time (Minutes)	Activity Clarifi- cations	Activity Classification			
				R	RR	RC	C
1. In-Person Meetings	————	60		—	—	—	—

If the total time you spent was routine, place an X in the "R" column; all 60 minutes are applied to routine work. If half the time was routine and half was creative, place an X under "R" and another under "C"; the time will be split evenly between the two classifications. Or you may decide to write in each category the actual minutes, percentages, or whatever is best for you. The survey process can accommodate whatever method is easy and convenient. Any unclear response will be clarified during the interview.

The "application" column gives you a place to record the activity or the application that was the subject of the meeting. Any information that will help you recall the purpose of this and the other activities in which you are involved goes on the WRM Activity Diary.

Activity Clarifications

Information ☐   Solve Problem ☐   Schedule ☐
Office ☐   Conference room ☐   Auditorium ☐
Scheduled ☐   Unscheduled ☐

As for the "activity clarifications" column shown above, suppose your manager walks into your office. He says, "I want you to explain the problem with the sales of [your product or service] year to date." The chances are you may not know the answer to this question. If you do not, the situation is obviously reactive-creative, and you may try to delay the meeting until you can be better prepared. If you know the answer, the situation is reactive-routine. You code this meeting as "Unscheduled," "Office," "Solve Problem."

Here's another example: You attend an announcement

meeting for a new stock investment program for all employees. How do you code this? The information is new and the
situation may be reactive-creative. As the meeting progresses,
some "old" information may be covered and the situation
becomes reactive-routine. What you record is your feeling
when each event occurs: "Scheduled," "Auditorium," "Information." Or you attend a department meeting to plan next
year's strategy. Your input is requested during the meeting.
In all probability you had advance notice of the meeting, so
initially it may appear to be a routine meeting. During the
meeting, however, many questions come up—some answers
are obvious, others are unknown. In your opinion, half the
meeting is routine and the other half is creative. As a result
you record the meeting as "Scheduled," "Conference room,"
"Solve Problem."

What happens if you have a second or third meeting in
a two-hour period? The overflow page, "Space for Recording
Multiple Activities," is for your convenience. On the left is a
two-hour time ladder and a section for notes. Use it any way
that will assist you to record the information. Because of the
space restriction, abbreviations are used for Scheduled
(Schd), Unscheduled (Unschd), Office (Off), Conference
room (CfR), Auditorium (Aud), Information (Inf), Solve
Problem (SP), and Schedule (Sdl).

Should a fourth meeting occur in the two-hour period,
there are blanks after the last "phone" item. The blanks can
also be used for an activity that is unique or that repeats an
activity covered in the activity log.

Telephone Calls

Activity Clarifications

Information ☐   Solve Problem ☐   Schedule ☐
In Company ☐   Out of Company ☐
      In/Out PhoneMail Messages No. _____

This item can also have multiple entries in a two-hour period. There is room on the overflow page for four additional calls. Once again, because of the space restriction, abbreviations are used for Information (Inf), Solve Problem (SP), Schedule (Sdl), In Company (IC), Out of Company (OC), and In/Out PhoneMail Messages No. (EMM. No.).

Let's look at three possible situations to illustrate how the same activity can be coded in different ways. (In the WRM process, it is not necessary to record every phone call. We use phone calls here just to illustrate a point.) First, you place a phone call: "Susan, would you arrange a flight to Orlando for Friday the 23rd? I will need a rental car and two nights' lodging." This is a routine situation. You code it as "Information," "In Company."

Second, you receive a call: "Dick, the budget review has been moved to one o'clock this afternoon. I know this is two weeks early, but please review your presentation with me at noon." This is a reactive situation for sure. If you are used to such meetings and know the format, content, and have prepared, then your presentation may be reactive-routine; if not, it may be reactive-creative. You code this phone call as "Information," "Solve Problem," "In Company." You classify this phone call as 70 percent routine and 30 percent creative, because the call was informative as well as problem solving.

Next, a phone call comes in: "Dick, I enjoyed the presentation but have a question. You indicated that a good office support management system should support creative work as well as routine. Is this applicable to financial analysts?" This is obviously a reactive situation. If you have to know something about financial analysts to answer this question and you don't have any experience with this type of work group, you would probably code the phone call reactive-creative. Or you may know a little about the work that financial analysts do and need to better understand the facts and think about them before answering. You code this call as "Solve Problem," "Out of Company." It was 100 percent creative for you.

Note: The "for you" is a very important point. You always

answer what type of situation each is for *YOU*. Don't worry how the situation may be coded by a colleague or the person you are talking to on the telephone.

There are two other interesting notes about phone calls. Let's assume you are a support person who occasionally relieves the switchboard. To record the switchboard phone calls, use the notes section on the overflow page; or use the first phone entry on that page to equal all routine phone traffic, and use hatch marks (////) to indicate the number of calls received. This could be important if the phone system is under consideration for a possible change.

You can use the second phone entry to record all reactive calls and a third phone entry to record all creative phone conversations. Also, notice the section marked EMM for Electronic Mail (or PhoneMail) Messages. If you prepare or read messages sent or received on a telephone answering system or an EMM, record them here. Many people do not know how much time is currently spent using these systems and would like such information for cost justification and system enhancement purposes. The studies to date indicate that around 12 to 15 percent of the workday is spent on EMM, thus telephone tag can be greatly diminished.

Working With Data

Activity Clarifications

No. Pages worked with _____   No. pages printed _____
Data entry ☐   Re-entry ☐   Revise ☐   Analysis ☐
Manual   ☐   (paper/pencil, calculator)
PC   ☐   (Intelligent workstation)
Host   ☐   (terminal to a mainframe)
Combined with: Text ☐   Graphics ☐   Other _____

Let's look at an example to determine how to use the clarifications list. Assume you are attempting to determine the quota for each of your sales personnel across the country for a new product. Your requirements are:

1. Four pages of data collected via telephone from remote sales offices
2. A calculator used to manipulate the numbers
3. Answers recorded in longhand
4. A text document that will be prepared
5. Graphs that will be needed

You check off "4 pages," "Revise," "Analysis," "Manual," "Combined with Text," and "Graphics." If this activity is a first-time effort, report this as a creative effort. On the other hand, if this is a repetitive quarterly process that you have on a spreadsheet, and the quota assignments are automatically filled out, you record it as a routine effort.

Working With Text

Activity Clarifications

No. Pages worked with _____ No. pages printed _____
Type ☐ Re-type ☐ Revise ☐ Originate text ☐
Manual ☐ (paper/pencil, longhand, typewriter)
WP ☐ (Wordprocessor, not PC compatible)
PC ☐ (WP software on the PC)
Host ☐ (WP software on a mainframe)
Combined with: Data ☐ Graphics ☐ Other _____

When working with text, the questions are very similar to working with data. However, the definitions are slightly different and a new category of a dedicated word processor (WP) is added.

Working With Graphics

Activity Clarifications

No. Pages worked with _____ No. pages printed _____
Draw   ☐   Re-draw ☐   Revise ☐   Design ☐
Manual   ☐   (paper/pencil, drafting board)
PC   ☐   (CAD on an intelligent workstation)
Host   ☐   (CAD on a mainframe)
Combined with: Text ☐   Data ☐   Other _____

These items are self-explanatory with the exception of
CAD, which stands for computer-aided design used by engineers.

Traveling and Moving, Waiting

These two items allow you to track the amount of time
spent moving about and waiting. They also allow you to
capture travel time within buildings, between locations in
town, and while on a trip.

Copying

This is copying you do yourself. Five copying jobs appear to be sufficient for a two-hour period for most people.
The most important information is the number of originals
and the number of copies per original. If you need additional room for additional copies, write the following in the
notes section so an accurate sizing of your copy needs can be
determined:

Job No.   1   2   3   4   5

No. originals   ___ ___ ___ ___ ___

No. copies/org. ___ ___ ___ ___ ___

If for any reason your copying exceeds five different combinations of originals and copy sets, duplicate this format on the overflow page and continue with job numbers 6, 7, 8, etc., as indicated below.

Job No.	6	7	8	9	10	Etc.	
No. originals	——	——	——	——	——	——	——
No. copies/org.	——	——	——	——	——	——	——

Filing, Retrieving

This activity is straightforward. The fill-in items are the number of files requested, the number you had time to look for, and the actual number of files found. The second set of items refers to the method used. Was it a manual search of file drawers? Did you use one of the many mechanical filing systems? Was the information filed or retrieved electronically via computer terminal?

Checking, Proofing

The format for this entry seems similar to the copying activity. You record the number of jobs checked, edited, and proofed. This work involves checking for sequence, content, coding, organization, errors, spelling, and the like.

Sorting, Assembling

In this activity, the first two questions identify associated volumes. The next questions refer to the most frequent associated activities performed.

Distribution, Mail

This information leads to understanding the networking and communications needs of the work group. The diagram on the page called "Daily Summary: Basic Format Types" (see the page after the last daily activity log) illustrates the format types most frequently disseminated. The document type reveals the relative intensity for alphabetic, numeric, annotated, graphic, and combination material. The chart on the "Output Distribution Log" page (see last page for day 1) asks the remaining questions essential to good network and distribution planning. For example, you supply the number of documents and number of pages to give the volume sensitivity.

The destination both within and outside the company gives the probability of internal networking versus outside assistance. The method of distribution gives a current time and cost picture, plus the format types already covered.

There are two critical areas of distribution. One is the formal distribution normally accomplished through the support personnel and the second is the informal, accomplished principal to principal. For example, someone sees your presentation and you give the person a copy (informal network). Someone asks you for data and you give it (informal network). Someone sends you an electronic note and asks for information. You key it and send it (informal network).

Managing/Supervising

"Managing" is confusing to most people. Most managers manage all day, in every activity. If you are working on a project in a meeting, someone is probably keeping the group on track—that is, the manager—and he or she is managing. If an employee comes to you for direction or with a question, that is managing. However, most managers record the latter as a meeting or an activity other than managing. That is fine; the WRM analysis is flexible.

There are times when you may feel the Managing/Supervising entry is especially warranted. There are two entries you may like to fill in. The first is "Managing Activity No. _____," and it refers to your involvement with activities labeled A through O (for 15 activities). For example, a meeting could be for one-on-one direction of a specific project. Your employee is analyzing a database to see how many employees are using the medical benefits package. She runs into two different ways the data may be assembled, and she needs your clarification. You may wish to record that you were helping the employee manage Activity C, to show where your management expertise is being used. In that case, you code it as "Managing Activity No. C," "Business Project."

A second example is an employee who has an appointment with you to discuss a morale problem, a job opportunity, or a raise in salary. Because this activity tends to align itself with a discrete management responsibility, you may correctly put this in the management category. Other discrete management tasks are career planning meetings, appraisals, and counseling sessions with employees.

Don't worry which category you use, however. The most important information is the recording of the activity that you are primarily engaged in.

Other Desk Work

There are a number of other activities we perform daily. Many times these are independent activities that are not associated with working with data, text, or graphics. When the activities occur independently of working on an overall application, they may be logged in this section of the two-hour activity log. The typical activities that fall into this category are as follows:

Activity Clarifications

Reading (not editing or revising) ☐
Listening ☐   Viewing ☐   Recording ☐
Thinking ☐   Planning ☐   Analyzing ☐
Schedule ☐   Calendar ☐   Control ☐

When any of these activities occur during work with text, data, and/or graphics, it is assumed that they are one of many activities grouped together to accomplish that work.

If you are involved in an activity that you feel does not fit a category on the two-hour activity log, write the activity down in the area provided on the overflow page after the last "2. Phone" entry and explain the activity in the "Notes" section.

Other Activities

In this section you include the following activities:

Activity Clarifications

Personal ☐   Breaks ☐   Lunch ☐
Emergency ☐   Medical ☐   Other _____

The Output Distribution Log

At the end of each day, there are two pages for recording the distribution of information. On the left-hand page are samples of document forms, such as narrative/text documents, statistical documents, forms, lists, and graphics. You identify the kind of document you've been working on and the form in which it will be distributed.

The right-hand page is the log itself. This is meant for finished work only. The number of documents in the example that follows is three. The total number of pages in the example that follows is twenty-six. You have sent three documents to various people in your workgroup. The first document is one page in length. The second document is ten pages in length. The third document is fifteen pages in length. The proper entry on the Output Distribution Log for that day would be:

Distribution Destination	Number of Documents	Number of Pages	Method of Distri- bution	Format Types 1 2 3 4 5
Your Company— Local				
A. Your Workgroup	3	26	C	√ √

It is this type of information you will need to determine the networking components for this particular work group and the volume of work transmitted. Respondents are asked to log all documents finished for a complete day and indicate the destination, number produced, and size. The respondent is also asked for the method of distribution and format type. If a combination is used, a percentage breakout should be supplied. This information helps you understand distribution points, volume, time sensitivity, and approximate current as well as future cost.

Appendix C

Work Redistribution Management Activity Diary

OFFICE ACTIVITY STUDY

Each two-hour period of the day you are to fill out a TWO HOUR ACTIVITY LOG. Although the forms may look complicated the first time you see them, most study participants find that after the first day, they take from one to five minutes to fill out the form. A group of principals will average about three activities per two-hour period. The office support personnel will average about eight activities per period.

The first two-hour period begins whenever you start work. For example, if your work day is from 9 to 5, you would complete a log at 11, 1, 3, and 5. The time you spend on breaks or lunch should be recorded under the last activity — "other." If you actually worked until 6:30 p.m., you would fill out a fifth log at 6:30 which would contain 90 minutes of activities.

The log sheet has four major sections. First, on the far left, is a list of the activities. Next, is a column in which you are to record the total number of minutes you spent engaged in that activity. The widest column, in the middle of the page, provides more detailed information on the activity. The right column classifies the type of work.

Some of the clarifications ask that you write a number (number of pages copied, number of items filed). Most of the clarifications can be filled out with a check mark. However, you may use the clarification spaces to record more detail. For example, you might have revised two one page letters and created one new one. Under "working with text" you would record "3" for number of pages and write 2 after "revise," and "1" after "Originate text." You would then place a check after "PC" if the work was done on a Personal Computer.

At the end of the day you complete the OUTPUT DISTRIBUTION LOG which indicates the method of distribution, format and classification of all finished documents.

FILLING OUT THE TWO-HOUR ACTIVITY LOG

The last column on the extreme right of the activity log may need some clarification. You are asked to classify each of your activities as R, RR, RC or C. There is no right or wrong answer to activity classification — you are the expert on your own activities. Your superior may review a summary of your coding as a check on the consistency of coding in the office. So that the classifications can be summarized for the entire office, you need to reach a common understanding of the four "pigeonholes" that are being used.

Routine	Reactive Routine	Reactive Creative	Creative
R	RR	RC	C

Classification "R" includes routine and repetitive work that is usually structured by standard procedures. Words that are associated with this classification are:

Routine	Repetitive	Structured	Planned
Required	Simple	Frequent	Common
Recurring	Delegable	Expected	Predictable

Classification "C" covers creative and unstructured work — for example, the first time an activity or application is done, a new way of looking at old information, seeing new possibilities, or accomplishing some task that may have to be done only once. Words associated with creative, unstructured, unique and innovative work are:

Creative	Unstructured	First time	Unique
Analysis	Investigate	Define	Study
Complex	Solution	Innovate	Improve
Research	Difficult	Proposal	Invent

Classifications "RR" and "RC" are for reactive work — tasks done under heavy time pressure. Under time pressure, either a routine or a creative reaction may be required. Words that often initiate reactive work are:

Reaction	Disruptive	Revision	Change
Cancellation	Expedite	Increase	Decrease
Delay	Deviation	Error	Oversight
Panic	Crisis	Do it now!	Quick fix

Therefore, each activity that a person accomplishes during the work day is to be placed into one of these four categories:

"R"	"C"
routine	creative
structured	unstructured
repetitive	first time, one of a kind
frequent	infrequent
can be scheduled	hard to schedule
delegable	not delegable
few elements	many elements, complex
simple	many interrelationships

"**RR**" Reactive Routine ("R" plus heavy time pressure, disruptive)
"**RC**" Reactive Creative ("C" plus heavy time pressure, disruptive)

The activity log is on the right hand page. Facing it on the left are two important recording aids. The first is a space for "notes." Here you may record notes on your activities as they occur against the 120 minute "time ladder." The notes can then be used to fill out the activity log at the end of the two-hour period.

The second aid is a "space for recording multiple activities" — an abbreviated version of the two-hour activity log. On this abbreviated log, you can record activities with the same activity number that have different activity classifications and/or clarifications.

For example, suppose that you were involved in eight phone calls, each about two minutes long. Assume that two calls were in each of the four different activity classifications (R, RR, RC, C). There are two ways you can record multiple classifications of the same activity:

1) If you wanted to indicate the classification with a check in one of the four columns, you would need four lines (rows) to record the four classifications. You can record the four kinds of calls using the line for activity 2 on the right, and three additional lines in abbreviated log on the left. The 16 minute total would be written in the "time" column.

(on the left)					(on the right)				
Activity	Time	R	RR	RC	C	Activity	Time	R	RR	RC	C
2	4		X			Phone	4	X			
2	4			X							
2	4				X						

2) If you prefer, you can use only one line by coding the total activity time under "time" and then indicating in each column, how much of the total should be allocated to each classification.

Activity	Time	R	RR	RC	C
Phone	16	4	4	4	4

TYPICAL WEEK — *Please estimate time spent on each activity in typical week*

Type of Activity	Estimated *Time Per Week* Spent On Activity	My Business Effectiveness Would *Definitely Improve* If I Were Able To Spend:	
		More Time On:	Less Time On:
1. *In person conversations, meetings* (Business — Not Dictation)	%	☐	☐
2. *Telephone conversations* (Business — Incoming and Outgoing)	%	☐	☐
3. *Working with Data*	%	☐	☐
4. *Working with Text*	%	☐	☐
5. *Working with Graphics*	%	☐	☐
6. *Traveling* (outside building)	%	☐	☐
7. *Moving about or Waiting* (within building for business purposes)	%	☐	☐
8. *Making copies*	%	☐	☐
9. *Searching/retrieving/filing materials*	%	☐	☐
10. *Checking or proofing materials*	%	☐	☐
11. *Sorting or Assembling materials*	%	☐	☐
12. *Mailing, Distribution, Delivery* (include messengers, Telex, FACS, hand-carried materials)	%	☐	☐
13. *Managing or Supervising personnel, activities or projects*	%	☐	☐
14. *Reading* (not for editing, revising)	%	☐	☐
15. *Listening* (tapes, recordings) or *Viewing* (film, slides)	%	☐	☐
16. *Thinking, planning, analyzing*	%	☐	☐
17. *Schedule, calendar, controls*	%	☐	☐
18. *Other Activities* (Lunch, Breaks, Medical, etc.)	%	☐	☐

Time should total 100%

Please Record Your Activities for Day 1

Day 1

Please record your activities for Day 1 in the pages that follow; the Time Ladder on the back of these pages may assist you in keeping track of daily activities.

Day 1 starts when you start work (i.e., 8:30 a.m., 9:00 a.m., etc.) and your first 2 hour period starts at the same time; include lunch and breaks in Activity 18, Other Activities.

Time Ladder *(for your convenience):*

	NOTES	SPACE FOR RECORDING MULTIPLE ACTIVITIES						
minutes		ACTIVITY number	TIME minutes	CLARIFICATION	R	RR	RC	C
Beginning of period — 0		1. MEET.		Inf ☐ SP ☐ Sdl ☐ Off ☐ CTR ☐ Aud ☐ Schd ☐ Unschd ☐				
— 5								
— 10		1. MEET.		Inf ☐ SP ☐ Sdl ☐ Off ☐ CTR ☐ Aud ☐ Schd ☐ Unschd ☐				
— 15								
— 20		2. PHONE		Inf ☐ SP ☐ Sdl ☐ IC ☐ OC ☐ EMM No. ___				
— 25								
— 30		2. PHONE		Inf ☐ SP ☐ Sdl ☐ IC ☐ OC ☐ EMM No. ___				
— 35								
— 40		2. PHONE		Inf ☐ SP ☐ Sdl ☐ IC ☐ OC ☐ EMM No. ___				
— 45								
— 50		2. PHONE		Inf ☐ SP ☐ Sdl ☐ IC ☐ OC ☐ EMM No. ___				
End of first hour — 55								
— 60		PROFS		Send ___ Receive ___				
— 65								
— 70								
— 75								
— 80								
— 85								
— 90								
— 95								
— 100								
— 105								
— 110								
— 115								
End of period — 120								

The "time ladder" is for your convenience in making notes of activities like a telephone interruption, a walk down the hall, a look in the files, a quick calculation, etc.) as they take place, so they are not overlooked at the end of the period when you fill in the summary on the opposite page. Use this "time bracket" in any way you find useful—it is not part of the record.

TWO HOUR ACTIVITY LOG

Date: _____ Ending time: _____

Beginning time: _____

Routine R
Reactive Routine RR
Reactive Creative RC
Creative C

ACTIVITY	APPLICATION	TIME (Minutes)	ACTIVITY CLARIFICATIONS	ACTIVITY CLASSIFICATION R	RR	RC	C
1. In-Person Meetings			Information ☐ Solve Problem ☐ Schedule ☐ Office ☐ Conference room ☐ Auditorium ☐ Scheduled ☐ Unscheduled ☐				
2. Telephone Calls			Information ☐ Solve Problem ☐ Schedule ☐ In Company ☐ Out of Company ☐ In/Out Phone/Mail Messages No. _____				
3. Working with Data			No. Pages worked with _____ No. pages printed _____ Data entry ☐ Re-entry ☐ Revise ☐ Analysis ☐ Manual ☐ (paper/pencil, calculator) PC ☐ (intelligent workstation) Host ☐ (terminal to a mainframe) Combined with: Text ☐ Graphics ☐ Other _____				
4. Working with Text			No. Pages worked with _____ No. pages printed _____ Type ☐ Re-type ☐ Revise ☐ Originate text ☐ Manual ☐ (paper/pencil, longhand, typewriter) WP ☐ (Wordprocessor, not PC compatible) PC ☐ (WP software on the PC) Host ☐ (WP software on a mainframe) Combined with: Data ☐ Graphics ☐ Other _____				
5. Working with Graphics			No. Pages worked with _____ No. pages printed _____ Draw ☐ Re-draw ☐ Revise ☐ Design ☐ Manual ☐ (paper/pencil, drafting board) PC ☐ (CAD on an intelligent workstation) Host ☐ (CAD on a mainframe) Combined with: Text ☐ Data ☐ Other _____				
6. Traveling			Local ☐ Overnight ☐ Other _____				
7. Moving, Waiting			Time Waiting, Minutes _____ Meeting cancelled ☐				
8. Copying			Job No. _____ 1 ☐ 2 ☐ 3 ☐ 4 ☐ 5 ☐ No. originals _____ No. copies/org. _____				
9. Filing, Retrieving			No. Filed _____ No. Looked for _____ No. Found _____ Manual ☐ PC ☐ Mainframe ☐				
10. Checking, Proofing			Job No. _____ 1 ☐ 2 ☐ 3 ☐ 4 ☐ 5 ☐ No. Pages _____				
11. Sorting, Assembling			No. Documents _____ No. Pages _____ Collate ☐ Tab ☐ Staple ☐ Punch ☐ Bind ☐ 3-Ring Binder ☐ Other _____				
12. Distribution, Mail			(Record Time Here. Use the OUTPUT DISTRIBUTION LOG for distribution details)				
13. Managing/Supervising			Managing Activity No. _____ and/or Personnel ☐ Business Project ☐ Other _____				
14. Other Desk Work			Reading (not editing or revising) ☐ Listening ☐ Viewing ☐ Recording ☐ Thinking ☐ Planning ☐ Analyzing ☐ Schedule ☐ Calendar ☐ Control ☐ Personal ☐ Breaks ☐ Lunch ☐ Emergency ☐ Medical ☐ Other ☐				
18. Other Activities							

Time Ladder *(for your convenience):*

	NOTES		SPACE FOR RECORDING MULTIPLE ACTIVITIES					
							CLASSIFICATION	
	minutes	ACTIVITY number	TIME minutes	CLARIFICATION		R	RR	RC	C
Beginning of period	0	1. MEET.		Inf ☐ SP ☐ Sdl ☐ / Off ☐ CRF ☐ Aud ☐ / Schd ☐ Unschd ☐					
	5								
	10	1. MEET.		Inf ☐ SP ☐ Sdl ☐ / Off ☐ CRF ☐ Aud ☐ / Schd ☐ Unschd ☐					
	15								
	20								
	25	2. PHONE		Inf ☐ SP ☐ Sdl ☐ / IC ☐ OC ☐ / EMM. No.					
	30								
	35								
	40	2. PHONE		Inf ☐ SP ☐ Sdl ☐ / IC ☐ OC ☐ / EMM. No.					
	45								
	50	2. PHONE		Inf ☐ SP ☐ Sdl ☐ / IC ☐ OC ☐ / EMM. No.					
	55								
End of first hour	60	2. PHONE		Inf ☐ SP ☐ Sdl ☐ / IC ☐ OC ☐ / EMM. No.					
	65								
	70								
	75	PROFS		Send / Receive					
	80								
	85								
	90								
	95								
	100								
	105								
	110								
	115								
End of period	120								

The "time ladder" is for your convenience in making notes of activities like a telephone interruption, a walk down the hall, a look in the files, a quick calculation, etc.) as they take place, so they are not overlooked at the end of the period when you fill in the summary on the opposite page. Use this "time bracket"in any way you find useful—it is not part of the record.

TWO HOUR ACTIVITY LOG

Date: _____
Beginning time: _____   Ending time: _____

Routine R
Reactive Routine RR
Reactive Creative RC
Creative C

ACTIVITY	APPLICATION	TIME (Minutes)	ACTIVITY CLARIFICATIONS	ACTIVITY CLASSIFICATION			
				R	RR	RC	C
1. In-Person Meetings			Information ☐ Solve Problem ☐ Schedule ☐ Office ☐ Conference room ☐ Auditorium ☐ Scheduled ☐ Unscheduled ☐				
2. Telephone Calls			Information ☐ Solve Problem ☐ Schedule ☐ In Company ☐ Out of Company ☐ In/Out PhoneMail Messages No. ____				
3. Working with Data			No. Pages worked with ____ No. pages printed ____ Data entry ☐ Re-entry ☐ Revise ☐ Analysis ☐ Manual ☐ (paper/pencil, calculator) PC ☐ (Intelligent workstation) Host ☐ (terminal to a mainframe) Combined with: Text ☐ Graphics ☐ Other ____				
4. Working with Text			No. Pages worked with ____ No. pages printed ____ Type ☐ Re-type ☐ Revise ☐ Originate text ☐ Manual ☐ (paper/pencil, longhand, typewriter) WP ☐ (Wordprocessor, not PC compatible) PC ☐ (WP software on the PC) Host ☐ (WP software on a mainframe) Combined with: Data ☐ Graphics ☐ Other ____				
5. Working with Graphics			No. Pages worked with ____ No. pages printed ____ Draw ☐ Re-draw ☐ Revise ☐ Design ☐ Manual ☐ (paper/pencil, drafting board) PC ☐ (CAD on an intelligent workstation) Host ☐ (CAD on a mainframe) Combined with: Text ☐ Data ☐ Other ____				
6. Traveling			Local ☐ Overnight ☐ Other ____				
7. Moving, Waiting			Time Waiting, Minutes ____ Meeting cancelled ☐				
8. Copying			Job No. 1 2 3 4 5 No. originals ____ No. copies/org. ____				
9. Filing, Retrieving			No. Filed ____ No. Looked for ____ No. Found ____ Manual ☐ PC ☐ Mainframe ☐				
10. Checking, Proofing			Job No. 1 2 3 4 5 No. Pages ____				
11. Sorting, Assembling			No. Documents ____ No. Pages ____ Collate ☐ Tab ☐ Staple ☐ Punch ☐ Bind ☐ 3-Ring Binder ☐ Other ____				
12. Distribution, Mail			(Record Time Here. Use the OUTPUT DISTRIBUTION LOG for distribution details)				
13. Managing/Supervising			Managing Activity No. ____ and/or Personnel ☐ Business Project ☐ Other ____				
14. Other Desk Work			Reading (not editing or revising) ☐ Listening ☐ Viewing ☐ Recording ☐ Thinking ☐ Planning ☐ Analyzing ☐ Schedule ☐ Calendar ☐ Control ☐				
18. Other Activities			Personal ☐ Breaks ☐ Lunch ☐ Emergency ☐ Medical ☐ Other ____				

Time Ladder *(for your convenience)*:

			SPACE FOR RECORDING MULTIPLE ACTIVITIES					
	NOTES	**ACTIVITY number**	**TIME minutes**	**CLARIFICATION**	**CLASSIFICATION**			
minutes					R	RR	RC	C
Beginning of period 0		1. MEET.		Inf ☐ SP ☐ Sdl ☐ Off ☐ CTR ☐ Aud ☐ Schd ☐ Unschd ☐				
5								
10								
15		1. MEET.		Inf ☐ SP ☐ Sdl ☐ Off ☐ CTR ☐ Aud ☐ Schd ☐ Unschd ☐				
20								
25		2. PHONE		Inf ☐ SP ☐ Sdl ☐ IC ☐ OC ☐ EMM No.				
30								
35		2. PHONE		Inf ☐ SP ☐ Sdl ☐ IC ☐ OC ☐ EMM No.				
40								
45								
50		2. PHONE		Inf ☐ SP ☐ Sdl ☐ IC ☐ OC ☐ EMM No.				
End of first hour 55								
60		2. PHONE		Inf ☐ SP ☐ Sdl ☐ IC ☐ OC ☐ EMM No.				
65								
70		PROFS		Send Receive				
75								
80								
85								
90								
95								
100								
105								
110								
End of period 115								
120								

The "time ladder" is for your convenience in making notes of activities like a telephone interruption, a walk down the hall, a look in the files, a quick calculation, etc.) as they take place, so they are not overlooked at the end of the period when you fill in the summary on the opposite page. Use this "time bracket" in any way you find useful—it is not part of the record.

TWO HOUR ACTIVITY LOG

Date: _____   Beginning time: _____   Ending time: _____

Routine R
Reactive Routine RR
Reactive Creative RC
Creative C

ACTIVITY	APPLICATION	TIME (Minutes)	ACTIVITY CLARIFICATIONS	ACTIVITY CLASSIFICATION			
				R	RR	RC	C
1. In-Person Meetings			Information [ ] Solve Problem [ ] Schedule [ ] Office [ ] Conference room [ ] Auditorium [ ] Scheduled [ ] Unscheduled [ ]				
2. Telephone Calls			Information [ ] Solve Problem [ ] Schedule [ ] In Company [ ] Out of Company [ ] In/Out PhoneMail Messages No. ___				
3. Working with Data			No. Pages worked with ___ No. pages printed ___ Data entry [ ] Re-entry [ ] Revise [ ] Analysis [ ] Manual [ ] (paper/pencil, calculator) PC [ ] (Intelligent workstation) Host [ ] (terminal to a mainframe) Combined with Text [ ] Graphics [ ] Other ___				
4. Working with Text			No. Pages worked with ___ No. pages printed ___ Type [ ] Re-type [ ] Revise [ ] Originate text [ ] Manual [ ] (paper/pencil, longhand, typewriter) WP [ ] (Wordprocessor, not PC compatible) PC [ ] (WP software on the PC) Host [ ] (WP software on a mainframe) Combined with Data [ ] Graphics [ ] Other ___				
5. Working with Graphics			No. Pages worked with ___ No. pages printed ___ Draw [ ] Re-draw [ ] Revise [ ] Design [ ] Manual [ ] (paper/pencil, drafting board) PC [ ] (CAD on an intelligent workstation) Host [ ] (CAD on a mainframe) Combined with Text [ ] Data [ ] Other ___				
6. Traveling			Local [ ] Overnight [ ] Other ___				
7. Moving, Waiting			Time Waiting, Minutes ___ Meeting cancelled [ ]				
8. Copying			Job No. ___ 1 2 3 4 5 No. originals ___ No. copies/org. ___				
9. Filing, Retrieving			No. Filed ___ No. Looked for ___ No. Found ___ Manual [ ] PC [ ] Mainframe [ ]				
10. Checking, Proofing			Job No. ___ 1 2 3 4 5 No. Pages ___				
11. Sorting, Assembling			No. Documents ___ No. Pages ___ Collate [ ] Tab [ ] Staple [ ] Punch [ ] Bind [ ] 3-Ring Binder [ ] Other ___				
12. Distribution, Mail			(Record Time Here, Use the OUTPUT DISTRIBUTION LOG for distribution details)				
13. Managing/Supervising			Managing Activity No. ___ and/or Personnel [ ] Business Project [ ] Other ___				
14. Other Desk Work			Reading (not editing or revising) [ ] Listening [ ] Viewing [ ] Recording [ ] Thinking [ ] Planning [ ] Analyzing [ ] Schedule [ ] Calendar [ ] Control [ ] Personal [ ] Breaks [ ] Lunch [ ] Emergency [ ] Medical [ ] Other [ ]				
18. Other Activities							

Time Ladder *(for your convenience)*:

	NOTES		SPACE FOR RECORDING MULTIPLE ACTIVITIES						
		ACTIVITY number	**TIME minutes**	**CLARIFICATION**		**CLASSIFICATION**			
minutes						**R**	**RR**	**RC**	**C**
Beginning of period — 0		1. MEET.		Inf ☐ SP ☐ Sdl ☐ Off ☐ CTR ☐ Aud ☐ Schd ☐ Unschd ☐					
— 5									
— 10		1. MEET.		Inf ☐ SP ☐ Sdl ☐ Off ☐ CTR ☐ Aud ☐ Schd ☐ Unschd ☐					
— 15									
— 20									
— 25		2. PHONE		Inf ☐ SP ☐ Sdl ☐ IC ☐ OC ☐ EMM. No. ____					
— 30									
— 35									
— 40		2. PHONE		Inf ☐ SP ☐ Sdl ☐ IC ☐ OC ☐ EMM. No. ____					
— 45									
— 50		2. PHONE		Inf ☐ SP ☐ Sdl ☐ IC ☐ OC ☐ EMM. No. ____					
End of first hour — 55									
— 60		2. PHONE		Inf ☐ SP ☐ Sdl ☐ IC ☐ OC ☐ EMM. No. ____					
— 65									
— 70									
— 75		PROFS		Send Receive					
— 80									
— 85									
— 90									
— 95									
— 100									
— 105									
— 110									
End of period — 115									
— 120									

The "time ladder" is for your convenience in making notes of activities like a telephone interruption, a walk down the hall, a look in the files, a quick calculation, etc.) as they take place, so they are not overlooked at the end of the period when you fill in the summary on the opposite page. Use this "time bracket" in any way you find useful—it is not part of the record.

TWO HOUR ACTIVITY LOG

Date: _____ Beginning time: _____ Ending time: _____

Routine — R
Reactive Routine — RR
Reactive Creative — RC
Creative — C

ACTIVITY	APPLICATION	TIME (Minutes)	ACTIVITY CLARIFICATIONS	ACTIVITY CLASSIFICATION R	RR	RC	C
1. In-Person Meetings			Information ☐ Solve Problem ☐ Schedule ☐ Office ☐ Conference room ☐ Auditorium ☐ Scheduled ☐ Unscheduled ☐	—	—	—	—
2. Telephone Calls			Information ☐ Solve Problem ☐ Schedule ☐ In Company ☐ Out of Company ☐ In/Out Phone/Mail Messages No. _____	—	—	—	—
3. Working with Data			No. Pages worked with _____ No. pages printed ☐ Data entry ☐ Re-entry ☐ Revise ☐ Analysis ☐ Manual ☐ (paper/pencil, calculator) PC ☐ ☐ (Intelligent workstation) Host ☐ ☐ (terminal to a mainframe) Combined with: Text ☐ Graphics ☐ Other _____	—	—	—	—
4. Working with Text			No. Pages worked with _____ No. pages printed ☐ Type ☐ Re-type ☐ Revise ☐ Originate text ☐ Manual ☐ (paper/pencil, longhand, typewriter) WP ☐ ☐ (Wordprocessor, not PC compatible) PC ☐ ☐ (WP software on the PC) Host ☐ ☐ (WP software on a mainframe) Combined with: Data ☐ Graphics ☐ Other _____	—	—	—	—
5. Working with Graphics			No. Pages worked with _____ No. pages printed ☐ Draw ☐ Re-draw ☐ Revise ☐ Design ☐ Manual ☐ (paper/pencil, drafting board) PC ☐ ☐ (CAD on an intelligent workstation) Host ☐ ☐ (CAD on a mainframe) Combined with: Text ☐ Data ☐ Other _____	—	—	—	—
6. Traveling			Local ☐ Overnight ☐ Other _____	—	—	—	—
7. Moving, Waiting			Time Waiting, Minutes _____ Meeting cancelled ☐	—	—	—	—
8. Copying			Job No. 1 2 3 4 5 No. originals _____ No. copies/org. _____	—	—	—	—
9. Filing, Retrieving			No. Filed _____ No. Looked for _____ No. Found _____ Manual ☐ PC ☐ Mainframe ☐	—	—	—	—
10. Checking, Proofing			Job No. 1 2 3 4 5 No. Pages _____	—	—	—	—
11. Sorting, Assembling			No. Documents _____ No. Pages _____ Collate ☐ Tab ☐ Staple ☐ Punch ☐ Bind ☐ 3-Ring Binder ☐ Other _____	—	—	—	—
12. Distribution, Mail			(Record Time Here. Use the OUTPUT DISTRIBUTION LOG for distribution details)	—	—	—	—
13. Managing/Supervising			Managing Activity No. _____ and/or Personnel ☐ Business Project ☐ Other _____	—	—	—	—
14. Other Desk Work			Reading (not editing or revising) ☐ Listening ☐ Viewing ☐ Recording ☐ Thinking ☐ Planning ☐ Analyzing ☐ Schedule ☐ Calendar ☐ Control ☐	—	—	—	—
18. Other Activities			Personal ☐ Breaks ☐ Lunch ☐ Emergency ☐ Medical ☐ Other ☐	—	—	—	—

Time Ladder (for your convenience):

SPACE FOR RECORDING MULTIPLE ACTIVITIES

	minutes	NOTES	ACTIVITY number	TIME minutes	CLARIFICATION	R	RR	RC	C
Beginning of period	0		1. MEET.		Inf ☐ SP ☐ Sdl ☐ Off ☐ CTR ☐ Aud ☐ Schd ☐ Unschd ☐				
	5								
	10		1. MEET.		Inf ☐ SP ☐ Sdl ☐ Off ☐ CTR ☐ Aud ☐ Schd ☐ Unschd ☐				
	15								
	20								
	25		2. PHONE		Inf ☐ SP ☐ Sdl ☐ IC ☐ OC ☐ EMM No. ___				
	30								
	35								
	40		2. PHONE		Inf ☐ SP ☐ Sdl ☐ IC ☐ OC ☐ EMM No. ___				
	45								
	50		2. PHONE		Inf ☐ SP ☐ Sdl ☐ IC ☐ OC ☐ EMM No. ___				
End of first hour	55								
	60		2. PHONE		Inf ☐ SP ☐ Sdl ☐ IC ☐ OC ☐ EMM No. ___				
	65								
	70								
	75		PROFS		Send ___ Receive ___				
	80								
	85								
	90								
	95								
	100								
	105								
	110								
	115								
End of period	120								

CLASSIFICATION: R RR RC C

The "time ladder" is for your convenience in making notes of activities like a telephone interruption, a walk down the hall, a look in the files, a quick calculation, etc.) as they take place, so they are not overlooked at the end of the period when you fill in the summary on the opposite page. Use this "time bracket" in any way you find useful—it is not part of the record.

TWO HOUR ACTIVITY LOG

Date: _____
Beginning time: _____ Ending time: _____

Routine — R
Reactive Routine — RR
Reactive Creative — RC
Creative — C

ACTIVITY	APPLICATION	TIME (Minutes)	ACTIVITY CLARIFICATIONS	ACTIVITY CLASSIFICATION R	RR	RC	C
1. In-Person Meetings			Information ☐ Solve Problem ☐ Schedule ☐ Office ☐ Conference room ☐ Auditorium ☐ Scheduled ☐ Unscheduled ☐				
2. Telephone Calls			Information ☐ Solve Problem ☐ Schedule ☐ In Company ☐ Out of Company ☐ In/Out PhoneMail Messages No. _____				
3. Working with Data			No. Pages worked with _____ No. pages printed _____ Data entry ☐ Re-entry ☐ Revise ☐ Analysis ☐ Manual ☐ (paper/pencil, calculator) PC ☐ (Intelligent workstation) Host ☐ (terminal to a mainframe) Combined with: Text ☐ Graphics ☐ Other _____				
4. Working with Text			No. Pages worked with _____ No. pages printed _____ Type ☐ Re-type ☐ Revise ☐ Originate text ☐ Manual ☐ (paper/pencil, longhand, typewriter) WP ☐ (Wordprocessor, not PC compatible) PC ☐ (WP software on the PC) Host ☐ (WP software on a mainframe) Combined with: Data ☐ Graphics ☐ Other _____				
5. Working with Graphics			No. Pages worked with _____ No. pages printed _____ Draw ☐ Re-draw ☐ Revise ☐ Design ☐ Manual ☐ (paper/pencil, drafting board) PC ☐ (CAD on an intelligent workstation) Host ☐ (CAD on a mainframe) Combined with: Text ☐ Data ☐ Other _____				
6. Traveling			Local ☐ Overnight ☐ Other _____				
7. Moving, Waiting			Time Waiting, Minutes _____ Meeting cancelled ☐				
8. Copying			Job No. 1 2 3 4 5 No. originals No. copies/org.				
9. Filing, Retrieving			No. Filed _____ No. Looked for _____ No. Found _____ Manual ☐ PC ☐ Mainframe ☐				
10. Checking, Proofing			Job No. 1 2 3 4 5 No. Pages				
11. Sorting, Assembling			No. Documents _____ No. Pages _____ Collate ☐ Tab ☐ Staple ☐ Punch ☐ Bind ☐ 3-Ring Binder ☐ Other _____				
12. Distribution, Mail			(Record Time Here. Use the OUTPUT DISTRIBUTION LOG for distribution details)				
13. Managing/Supervising			Managing Activity No. _____ and/or Personnel ☐ Business Project ☐ Other _____				
14. Other Desk Work			Reading (not editing or revising) ☐ Listening ☐ Viewing ☐ Recording ☐ Thinking ☐ Planning ☐ Analyzing ☐ Schedule ☐ Calendar ☐ Control ☐				
18. Other Activities			Personal ☐ Breaks ☐ Lunch ☐ Emergency ☐ Medical ☐ Other _____				

DAILY SUMMARY

BASIC FORMAT TYPES

1. <u>NARRATIVE/TEXT:</u>
   Letters/Memos
   Reports/Proposals
   Strategies/Analysis
   Manuals

2. <u>STATISTICAL:</u>
   Tables/Analysis
   Computer Runs
   General Ledger
   Inventories
   Price Lists

3. <u>FORMS:</u>
   Bills/Invoices
   Purchase Orders
   Applications
   Time Cards
   Expense Accounts

4. <u>LISTS:</u>
   Parts Lists
   Reference Manuals
   Price Lists
   Directories
   Notification

5. <u>GRAPHICS:</u>
   Foils/Charts
   Organization
   Charts
   Flow Charts
   Forecasts
   Presentations
   Drawings

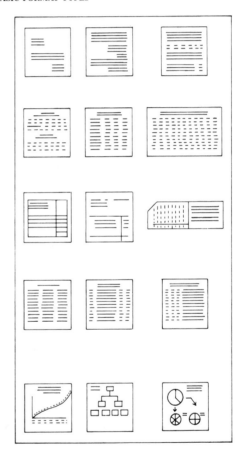

OUTPUT DISTRIBUTION LOG
FINISHED WORK ONLY

DISTRIBUTION DESTINATION	NUMBER OF DOCUMENTS	NUMBER OF PAGES	METHOD OF DISTRIBUTION	FORMAT TYPES				
				1	2	3	4	5
YOUR COMPANY — LOCAL								
A. YOUR WORKGROUP								
B. YOUR DEPARTMENT								
C. ANOTHER DEPARTMENT								
YOUR COMPANY — DISTANT								
D. SAME CITY								
E. ANOTHER CITY								
F. ANOTHER STATE								
G. ANOTHER COUNTRY								
ANOTHER COMPANY								
H. CLIENT								
I. CUSTOMER								
J. SUPPLIER								
K. OTHER _____								

METHOD OF DISTRIBUTION

A) Electronic Mail
B) Hand Carried
C) Company Mail
D) U.S. Mail
E) Courier

F) Special Delivery
G) Telex
H) FACS
I) Other _____

FORMAT TYPES

1) Narrative/text
2) Statistical/tables
3) Forms
4) Lists
5) Graphics

Please Record Your Activities for Day 2

Day 2

Please record your activities for Day 2 in the pages that follow; the Time Ladder on the back of these pages may assist you in keeping track of daily activities.

Day 2 starts when you start work (i.e., 8:30 a.m., 9:00 a.m., etc.) and your first 2 hour period starts at the same time; include lunch and breaks in Activity 18, Other Activities.

Repeat five sets of "Space for Recording Multiple Activities" sheets and "Two Hour Activity Logs," a "Daily Summary: Basic Format Types," and an "Output Distribution Log."

Please Record Your Activities for Day 3

Day 3

Please record your activities for Day 3 in the pages that follow; the Time Ladder on the back of these pages may assist you in keeping track of daily activities.

Day 3 starts when you start work (i.e., 8:30 a.m., 9:00 a.m., etc.) and your first 2 hour period starts at the same time; include lunch and breaks in Activity 18, Other Activities.

Repeat five sets of "Space for Recording Multiple Activities" sheets and "Two Hour Activity Logs," a "Daily Summary: Basic Format Types," and an "Output Distribution Log."

Please Record Your Activities for Day 4

Day 4

Please record your activities for Day 4 in the pages that follow; the Time Ladder on the back of these pages may assist you in keeping track of daily activities.

Day 4 starts when you start work (i.e., 8:30 a.m., 9:00 a.m., etc.) and your first 2 hour period starts at the same time; include lunch and breaks in Activity 18, Other Activities.

Repeat five sets of "Space for Recording Multiple Activities" sheets and "Two Hour Activity Logs," a "Daily Summary: Basic Format Types," and an "Output Distribution Log."

Please Record Your Activities for Day 5

Day 5

Please record your activities for Day 5 in the pages that follow; the Time Ladder on the back of these pages may assist you in keeping track of daily activities.

Day 5 starts when you start work (i.e., 8:30 a.m., 9:00 a.m., etc.) and your first 2 hour period starts at the same time; include lunch and breaks in Activity 18, Other Activities.

Repeat five sets of "Space for Recording Multiple Activities" sheets and "Two Hour Activity Logs," a "Daily Summary: Basic Format Types," and an "Output Distribution Log."

Notes

Chapter 2

1. Rosabeth Moss Kanter, "Office Automation and People: A New Dimension" (A study prepared for Honeywell, October 1983); and Rosabeth Moss Kanter, "Computers Should Be Head Tools, Not Hand Tools," *Management Review*, April 1986.
2. Douglas Murray McGregor, "The Human Side of the Enterprise," *Management Review*, November 1957.
3. A. H. Maslow, *Motivation and Personality* (New York: Harper & Row, 1954).

Chapter 6

1. Peter Drucker, *Management Tasks, Reponsibilities, Practices* (New York: Harper & Row, 1979).

Chapter 8

1. Serge A. Birn, Richard M. Crossan, and Ralph W. Eastwood, *Measurement and Control of Office Costs* (New York: McGraw-Hill, 1961).
2. Maynard, Stegmarten, and Schwab, *Methods-Time Measurement (MTM)* (New York: McGraw-Hill, 1948).
3. Birn, Crossan, and Eastwood, *Measurement and Control.*
4. Birn, Crossan, and Eastwood, *Measurement and Control.*

Part II

1. Peter G. Sassone and A. Perry Schwartz, "Cost Justifying OA," *Datamation*, February 15, 1987.

Glossary

The following are words and phrases used frequently in this book. Each is defined when discussed in the text, but these quick glossary definitions may be useful for easy reference.

activity A physical or mental effort; a series of activities may result in an observable application.

application The final stage of a series of activities or a business process, usually in the form of a tangible result or product.

augmentation The use of something that improves our ability to perform a first-time work effort, or an infrequent or unpredictable work activity with low volume.

automation The mechanization of a pre-determined sequence of repetitive work activities that have volume and repetition as a substitute for human effort.

basic work facilities Software tools that augment work activities in the five business functions (access to information, problem solving, documentation, distribution, and communication) and support the different types of work (routine, reactive, and creative).

Benevolent Theory X A management style best suited for routine work that emphasizes respect for the individual and uses recognition and incentives to reward outstanding performance.

business application The final stage of a business process or a series of activities that may require either automation or augmentation to make the process more efficient or effective.

business process A defined, known set of activities and resulting applications.

business strategy A plan of action to accomplish the visionary expectations of an enterprise, which includes (at a minimum) an understanding of one's customers, products/services, competitive forces, and how to best utilize internal and market resources for optimum competitive advantage or public service.

creative work A first-time, one-of-a-kind, or infrequent effort to define and understand an idea, problem, or opportunity and to develop a solution.

CPU Central Processing Unit, usually referring to a computer mainframe.

data Information in the form of numbers, text, graphics, voice, and image.

data facilities Those augmentation tools that support two of the five business functions—access to information and problem solving.

data processing The storing or processing of raw data by a computer.

data processing applications A set of observable reports or displays that result from automating a known business process.

document preparation The activity of transferring one's thoughts, ideas, or analysis to some documented form.

document processing A system of producing typewritten documents by use of automated typewriters and electronic text editing equipment.

effectiveness Doing things better; creatively modifying and improving an existing set of activities, applications, products, and/ or services to produce more desirable results for the first time.

efficiency Doing things faster; performing a repetitive set of high-volume activities and/or applications with less resources (time, energy, or money).

facility An augmentation software tool.

fixed function terminal A CRT with limited internal intelligence that interacts with a CPU, also referred to as a "dumb" terminal or MFI (mainframe interactive) terminal.

foundation facilities A set of augmentation software tools (14 +) that support the five business functions to increase white-collar productivity.

function A logical grouping of work activities commonly found in an office environment.

hierarchy of needs A. H. Maslow's list of needs describing the sequential priority of motivating factors for individuals in a work environment.

innovation Doing new things; creating an entirely new set of activities, applications, products, or services for the first time.

intelligent workstation A PC-like device with the internal capacity and intelligence to perform computing independent of a CPU, or which can be networked with other CPUs and/or PC-type devices.

keyboarding A term that describes the act of typing on a keyboard by principals; this term is used because it is psychologically more palatable to principals than the term "typing."

LAN Local Area Network.

line-of-business application An automated data processing application that primarily benefits a department or business unit and is usually characterized as having high-volume, repetitive, transaction-oriented processing.

office A place to work; a work environment where predominantly white-collar work is performed.

office applications A tangible result of a series of activities occurring in a work environment called the office.

PEP People, Equipment, Procedures.

power The ability to influence someone's behavior to accomplish a desired, specific objective.

principal An executive, manager, or professional who is paid primarily to accomplish creative work.

process A system of operations used in the production of something; a series of actions or changes that bring about an end or result.

reactive work Work that is disruptive in nature and has time constraints because of its urgency or importance.

relational data base A table-driven architecture for a data base that allows users to more simply define the parameters for extracting and working with data; one of three primary data architectures, the others being "network" and "hierarchical."

routine work Work that is highly repetitive, predictable, and with high volume; routine work is usually delegable to administrative and clerical support personnel.

support personnel Administrative and clerical personnel who are paid primarily to accomplish recurring, delegable, routine work.

Theory X   Douglas M. McGregor's management philosophy based on the assumption that people would be passive, even resistant, with regard to organizational needs without management intervention because workers basically lack ambition and are irresponsible.

Theory Y   Douglas M. McGregor's management philosophy based on the assumption that people are not, by nature, passive or resistant to organizational needs, but on the contrary, motivation exists in all workers if given the opportunity to align their own self-fulfillment needs with the goals of the company.

vision   A clear image or framework defined and communicated by the chief executive, which guides those strategic choices that will determine the future nature and direction of an enterprise or establishment.

work   Effort expended to accomplish activities and applications.

work group   The smallest identifiable element in an organization with a common manager and whose members share a common objective, with a strong need to communicate among themselves.

Further Reading

The theories presented in this book are grounded in management principles that have evolved over the years. The following outstanding publications reflect these principles. Included are our comments on how they relate to *The White-Collar Shuffle*.

1. Lynda M. Applegate, James I. Cash, Jr., and D. Quinn Mills, "Information Technology and Tomorrow's Manager," *Harvard Business Review*, Vol. 66, No. 6 (November–December 1988).

   The authors explain how Information Technology (IT) is being used to: (1) change organizational structures by blurring the distinctions between centralization and decentralization, (2) change management processes by separating control from reporting relationships and by supporting more creativity, and (3) changing human resources by changing job responsibilities and descriptions, and making the workers better trained and more autonomous.

2. Joel Arthur Barker, *Discovering the Future: The Business of Paradigms*. St. Paul, Minn.: ILI Press, 1988.

   Mr. Barker explains that paradigms are existing sets of rules or regulations. They define our boundaries and, therefore, can restrict our strategies for success, our creativity, our vision, and our willingness to take risks, because they act as filters that mask innovative ideas that do not align with existing expectations. In effect, a paradigm is our comfortable, routine environment, and creative energy is needed to disrupt it. Sometimes the disruption that results from new ideas is extremely uncomfortable, causing tremendous resistance to change. But when new paradigms are discovered, according to Mr. Barker, traditional frames of reference can be totally replaced by a new set of rules, and everyone affected "goes back to zero." In *The White-Collar Shuffle*, we are recommending a new paradigm to revolutionize white-collar productivity by utilizing a new management philosophy, a new framework for utilizing augmentation technology tools, and a new methodology to measure and redistribute work. We recommend that management take a new approach to address current downsizing challenges, remove the bureaucratic weight of existing organizations, and nourish a work environment where the creation of new paradigms flourish.

3. Steve Buchholz and Thomas Roth, *Creating the High Performance Team*. New York: John Wiley, 1987.

This book provides an excellent review of the essentials for building high performance teams, the role of participative management, and the synergistic leverage of both strong corporate cultures and vision. The authors explain how high performance teams can be dynamically created and disbanded for specific tasks. Traditionally, team members worked in close proximity to one another, but in the future, the necessary team member skills will be more geographically dispersed. In *The White-Collar Shuffle*, we explain the need for a common, electronic augmentation platform that will facilitate sharing of these skills across organizational boundaries, which link team members together as they dynamically shift roles, responsibilities, and physical locations.

4. Peter F. Drucker, *Management Tasks, Responsibilities, Practices*. New York: Harper & Row, 1979.

As it relates to *The White-Collar Shuffle*, we recommend the section on "Productive Work and the Achieving Worker," which includes Chapters 15–23. Specifically, in Chapter 17 ("Making Work Productive: Work and Process") and Chapter 21 ("The Responsible Worker"), we completely agree with Drucker's observation that the knowledge worker is not productive in a coercive environment, but is stimulated by self-motivation and self-direction. However, we do not totally agree with his statement that "we cannot truly define, let alone measure, productivity for most knowledge work." And although we agree with his view that "making work productive has to start out with the end product, the output of work," we would add that it also must start with a clear understanding of routine, reactive, and creative work, and whether management is getting the right work to the right people. And finally, we also agree with his comment that determining what tools (skills, information, and knowledge) need to be applied to work activities "must always be determined by the end product" desired. This is quite simple to determine for routine work, but more difficult when addressing the creative work process. In *The White-Collar Shuffle*, we point out that traditional automation technology is appropriate when the end product is known and has predictable volume. But when the end product itself is unknown (creative work), when the volume and sequence of desired activities are somewhat unclear or not yet defined from previous work experiences, then augmentation technology tools can best boost productivity.

5. Barbara Garson, *The Electronic Sweatshop*. New York: Simon and Schuster, 1988.

   This can be a rather depressing book at times, but it is worth reading. It's depressing in the sense that the author cites how technology in the office has sometimes further specialized and dehumanized many tasks similarly to the way automation and other technologies affected factories during the industrial revolution. She gives examples where management's choice of office technology appeared to be insensitive to its potential dehumanizing impact, mainly because of the philosophy that assumes people are lazy and stupid (Theory X approach). But this book is worth reading. It provides further evidence of our view in *The White-Collar Shuffle* as to why all work cannot be treated the same, why work in the office environment cannot be managed like work in the factory, why a Benevolent Theory X (at best) is more appropriate than a traditional hard-line Theory X mentality, why a Theory Y approach is more effective for building high-performance cultures, and why common augmentation tool platforms are essential to support the dynamic redistribution of work in the office and, thereby, provide greater challenges and self-fulfillment.

6. Cyrus Gibson and Barbara Bund Jackson, *The Information Imperative*. Lexington, Mass.: D. C. Heath and Company, Lexington Books, 1987.

   The authors describe how technologies are transforming the way people work, but warn that "real office productivity comes from changing the work itself, and that has nothing to do with technology." The book reviews how information technology (IT) impacts customer relationships, channel of distribution, competitive forces, etc. But the two chapters that complement some thoughts in *The White-Collar Shuffle* are Chapters 2 and 7. Chapter 2 describes how transaction processing in the 1970s (automation of routine work) delivered benefits to specific functional units of an organization (accounting, purchasing, personnel, etc.), how end user computing in the early 1980s delivered benefits to the individuals, and why the new challenge is to apply technology in a way that transforms the organization itself. Chapter 7 further discusses the concept of integrating technology to make this transformation. In *The White-Collar Shuffle*, we show how a better understanding of work itself, augmentation technology, and a new measurement and management methodology can help redistribute work to support this continual transformation process.

7. Craig Hickman and Michael Silva, *Creating Excellence: Managing Corporate Culture, Strategy and Change in the New Age*. New York: Plume, 1984.

The authors contrast the old age of management, strategy, and culture with the new and discuss the importance of vision. They itemize new age executive skills and their link to building successful cultures. This book contains numerous self-assessment checklists on such items as one's vision, executive insight, patience, focus, versatility, and cultural awareness. It provides an interesting framework for analyzing one's commitment to adapt to increasing demands to change the culture of work environments to maximize innovation and white-collar productivity.

8. Rosabeth Moss Kanter, *When Giants Learn to Dance*. New York: Simon and Schuster, 1989.

The author discusses the challenges in the corporate global "Olympics" of the 1990s in terms of new strategies, new management and leadership skills, organizational structures, and social dilemmas. We particularly recommend the following chapters as they relate to some themes in *The White-Collar Shuffle*. Chapter 3 describes the perils of restructuring and downsizing, and the associated threats to productivity and creativity. Chapter 4 further explains the need for a "thoughtful restructuring versus mindless downsizing," specifically, why departmental contributions must be measured and differentiated, how "anorexic companies" can "starve innovation," and three keys to increase synergy. And Chapter 10 describes the tension and challenges that occur when "newstream" ideas and concepts (creative work-oriented) must fight the "mainstream" (routine work-oriented) management. Bureaucracies support mainstream historical activities that are routine and that they feel comfortable with. But new ideas (creative work) require fluid team-oriented relationships and organizations. So "newstream needs (creative work) and mainstream management (routine) are thus in conflict." (The words in parentheses are ours.)

9. Harold J. Leavitt, *Corporate Pathfinders*. New York: Penguin Books, 1987.

   Mr. Leavitt makes a stimulating distinction between people within an organization who may be "pathfinders," "problem solvers," and "implementors" and explains why we need all three. Pathfinders are visionary leaders whose role is to ask the right questions, to communicate their vision, to inspire others to become believers, and to be persistent. The problem solver's role is to get the right answers, to apply logic and rational thinking, and to provide evidence. And the implementor's role is to get the right things done through people. Leavitt defines the characteristics of pathfinders and the organizational culture needed to support them. Interestingly, he also explains why most universities and colleges produce problem solvers rather than the pathfinders we so desperately need and shares his ideas on teaching vision and creativity.

10. Dean N. Meyer and Mary E. Boone, *The Information Edge*. New York: McGraw-Hill, 1987.

    The authors define office automation (OA) as "computer and communications-based tools for thinking" and clearly make the distinction between unstructured knowledge work and traditional, routine data processing operational business applications. They give a number of case histories where OA tools for thinking have produced value-added benefits and explain the difficulty of using traditional justification approaches for knowledge-worker technology investments.

11. Henry Mintzberg, *The Structuring of Organizations*. Englewood Cliffs, N.J.: Prentice-Hall, 1979.

12. Kenichi Ohmae, *The Mind of the Strategist.* New York: McGraw-Hill, 1987.

    As a director of McKinsey & Company, Mr. Ohmae explains why many of today's institutions are not organized to stimulate strategic thinking or leverage innovation, but rather too often to tie success to conformity. He contrasts true strategic thinking with mechanical or linear thinking and intuition, and explains why a focus on key success factors is critical to breaking new ground and removing these obstacles. In *The White-Collar Shuffle*, we stress the need to stop wasting our potential for innovative brain power and explain why technology in itself is not the only success factor when addressing the office productivity issue, but why a new management understanding about the dynamics of work is key.

13. Tom Peters, *Thriving on Chaos.* New York: Harper & Row, 1987.

    This management book is a must for re-thinking traditional management philosophies, customer relationships, and leadership. It preaches empowerment and trust of the worker, participative management and incentives, and elimination of bureaucratic deadweight. As it relates to *The White-Collar Shuffle*, we specifically recommend Chapter I–10 ("Create a Corporate Capacity for Innovation"), the entire "P" section ("Achieving Flexibility by Empowering People"), Chapters L–2 ("Develop an Inspiring Vision"), S–2 ("Revamp the Chief Controls"), and S–3 ("Decentralize Information, Authority and Strategic Planning").

14. John F. Rockart and David W. DeLong, *Executive Support Systems.* Homewood, Ill.: Dow Jones-Irwin, 1988.

    We recommend Chapter 3 ("ESS and the Nature of Executive Work") to broaden one's theoretical perspective on aspects of work. In *The White-Collar Shuffle*, we describe a common foundation of augmentation tools based on the way people work and suggest that it could be a platform for building a customized Executive Support System. Our list of tools is somewhat broader than those defined in Chapter 4 by Rockart and DeLong, but is quite similar in the desired basic functions of a good ESS. We also highly recommend Chapter 7 ("Implementation: Overview and Sponsorship Roles"), which emphasizes the criticality of executive commitment when implementing technology tools that tremendously enhance top management's decision-making process and access to information.

15. Ralph H. Sprague, Jr. and Eric D. Carlson, *Building Effective Decision Support Systems.* Englewood Cliffs, N.J.: Prentice-Hall, 1982.

16. Robert Tomasko, *Downsizing: Reshaping the Corporation for the Future.* New York: AMACOM, 1990.

In *The White-Collar Shuffle*, we emphasize that reversing the downward trend in white-collar productivity will require a re-examination of: (1) the nature of office work, (2) current reactive downsizing actions, (3) the new roles of managers and different management styles, (4) the impact of technology on organizational design, and (5) a distinction between the use of automation and augmentation technology. Tomasko reviews the underlying forces of the demassing we have witnessed in the late 1980s. He compares the unfavorable management bulge in the U.S. business arena to the situation in other nations. He explains some reasons for the existing excessive management layers and the negative impact this bulge can have on one's competitive posture. Downsizing benefits, approaches, principles, and human resources strategies to stay streamlined are covered. We especially agree with his comment in Chapter 4 that "too many companies embark on overhead reduction efforts loosely targeted at middle management." But we are also quite distressed at the continued emphasis on reducing administrative support. Such downsizing threatens to turn professionals and managers into routine administrators who have little time to do the creative work they were hired to perform. It is in Chapter 4 that Tomasko discusses the important distinction between problems caused by too many layers of management versus excessive professional staff. He concludes by outlining the strengths and weaknesses of eight general approaches for reviewing staff downsizing potential. The WRM approach in *The White-Collar Shuffle* combines the best aspects of the activity analysis approach mentioned, along with the advantages of the staff-value analysis approach discussed. In addition, WRM provides a management framework for the ongoing measurement and redistribution of work performed in the office.

17. Benjamin Tregoe, John Zimmerman, Ronald Smith, and Peter Tobia, *Vision in Action.* New York: Simon and Schuster, 1989.

With numerous examples from their experience, the authors explain how strategic visions are created and translated into reality by achieving the necessary participation. Their writings complement some of the thoughts in Harold Leavitt's earlier book, *Corporate Pathfinders.* Some of the authors' helpful advice includes five key questions for clarifying your vision, a summary of distinctions between vision (including supporting strategies) and operations, a discussion about the process of integrating vision into operations, and a list of eight key variables, usually driving forces within corporations that heavily influence or determine their strategic choices. In *The White-Collar Shuffle*, we briefly discuss the critical need for vision to be communicated from the top of the organization to its lowest element. We also describe a new vision for office productivity that can be a shot of adrenalin to enhance our creativity and competitiveness.

18. Shoshana Zuboff, *In the Age of the Smart Machine.* New York: Basic Books, 1988.

Tracing the origin of white-collar work and the roles of executives, managers, and clerical workers, the author reviews the underlying hopes of management when applying automation and its frequent dehumanizing impact. She also explains how new "informating" technology may now empower workers, changing not only their work gratification and responsibilities but also the traditional role of management. As mentioned in *The White-Collar Shuffle*, we have very little doubt that it will revolutionize management's role and traditional lines of authority relationships. The author's description of the frustrating automation that occurs in the office is the traditional use of technology that we refer to as automation of routine work. And her description of using technology to "informate" office work is similar in concept to our description of empowering office workers with a common platform of augmentation technology tools. We agree with her thoughts about how "informating" technology can dramatically transform office work and employee satisfaction through broadened responsibilities and can also become a source of positive empowerment.

Index